#DearChristianMen

Going beyond casual Christianity and hypocrisy in the Church

C.J. Greiner

#DearChristianMen

Edited by Holly Fisher

Cover Design by CreateSpace

Printed by CreateSpace

Published by CJ Greiner

Printed in the United States of America

ISBN: 0692439005
ISBN-13: 978-0692439005

DEDICATION

To my beautiful fiancé and future wife.

You are such a blessing to me and others around you.

I am honored to spend the rest of my life with you.

I love you.

#DearChristianMen

CONTENTS

#DearChristianMen

ACKNOWLEDGMENTS

I would like to thank a special group of people who made all this possible. Thank you to my mother who loves me with everything she has. Your support and love for me doesn't go unnoticed. I want to thank my father and step-mom (Larry and Ruby). Thank you for always loving Leana and I. Your joyful giving encourages us every day. Thank you to my wonderful mother-in-law, Irma Rivera (my Madre) and her constant support and encouragement. Special thanks to my father-in-law, Ramon Rivera. Your generosity is overwhelming and I thank you for your love and support. You show me what a real man of God is all about. Thank you Allison Vogel who constantly encouraged me and prayed for me. God used you to really push this project forward. Thank you to my pastor, Mark Driscoll, for preaching and teaching the Word of God with boldness. Your passion for God is evident by all who have heard you preach. Thank you for never watering down God's Word. Big thanks to Holly Fisher for editing this book. Your time and effort has been such a blessing to us. I want to thank my best friend, Hunter Driscoll. Thank you for your obedience to God. Your friendship means the world to me. And to a special friend who wants to remain anonymous, thank you for your financial support and your encouragement.

I want to thank my New Life Fellowship family for teaching me what true love and community is all about. You have forever blessed me.

Thank you, Leana Rivera, for being the love of my life. Your daily encouragement has helped me mature over the years. Your constant love and faith in me has caused me to go above and beyond anything I ever thought I could. God uses you daily to remind me of all the blessings I have.

Thank you to those who blessed this project financially:

Ethan Barlow	Edith Beery
Allison Vogel	Cristina Perez
Ramon and Irma Rivera	Cherri Fuehring
Anonymous	LeAnn Stark
Anonymous	Chris Bischof
Scotty Campbell	Elvira Galvez
Miguel Palmerin	Brenda Ortiz

Thank you to all of you who gave. You gave above and beyond anything I could ever ask. I am so humbled by all your generosity and support. God used every single one of you to make this idea into a reality.

#DEARCHRISTIANMEN

INTRODUCTION

#DearChristianMen,

I heard this story of a man who owned a factory. This factory had a lot of employees but only few who have actually been there for more than a year. Men and women would come and go within months, weeks and even days of working there. The problem was that so many of those people wanted the check but did not want to work. The owner was to the point where he would hire anyone, no matter the experience, just as long as they wanted to work. "I just want them to show up and have a desire to work. I would give them all the training they needed," the man said. When I first heard this I immediately thought of the body of Christ. I thought of many Christian men. I even thought of who I used to be, even who I still can be sometimes.

All throughout the Bible, you see men and women going through the motions of "Christianity" but never really letting it become their lifestyle; never really letting it become more than just a religion. They wanted the benefits of maturity without going through the process of growing up. This is exactly what is happening now. We want a paycheck but don't want to put forth the effort. We want to go deeper with God, but we don't even do the simple things He has called us to do.

"*I desire obedience over sacrifice*" God said this to His people in **Isaiah 1** and **1 Samuel 15**. Much like this business owner's words, God didn't want their sacrifices and offerings; He wanted their heart. He wanted their obedience. He wanted their devotion. This business man would have taken someone without experience, as long as they were willing to learn, grow, and be obedient. God wants the same thing. As long as your heart is willing to submit, then God can use you and mold you into the man of God you were called to be.

We need you

#DearChristianMen,

I am writing this to you because the world needs you. I am writing this to you because the world needs us. I myself was once lost, but by the grace of God I have been found. I know what the other side looks like. And I now know what my purpose is: to wake you up.

#DearChristianMen, I am writing this to you because the Body of Christ needs you. I am writing this because this world lacks real men who truly show themselves as men. #DearChristianMen, I am writing this to you because our women need you. They do not need your empty promises, they do not need your muscles, they do not need your body, and they surely do not need your money. They need leaders to lead, fathers to teach, and warriors to fight for them. #DearChristianMen, our children need you. They need a real man to look up to. They need to know how to act, how to love, and how to respect. They need an earthly father to show them how to live for God. They need to know what is right and what is wrong. The world does not need any more boys, it needs men.

#DearChristianMen, God needs you. He created men with a purpose to lead, and without that leadership the women will have to step up to take on a spot they were never meant to fulfill. God doesn't need us for Him to exist, He needs us to be what He created us to be... Men... Real men. Men that are not afraid. Men who treat women with respect; who protect their purity. Men who teach their children how to live and act. Men who are not afraid to stand up for what they believe. God needs men to lead His people. Men who are present. Men who are active. Men who put their needs aside to provide for their wives and kids. Men who don't look at women as objects of satisfaction. Men of faith who are not moved by the storms of life. We need men who display true faith in God. Men who will not form to the patterns of this world. We need men who are sanctified and set apart. We need men who know their purpose.

No more casual Christians

Men, we live in a world where believing in God has become casual. We treat God like our homie, who is cool with whatever we do. Or we treat Him like He is too distant to know. Although He is our Father and we are His children, we have lost true reverence towards our Maker. What happened to truly falling on our faces in prayer? What happened to going to church out of eagerness to learn more, not because we were forced or because it's the "right" thing to do? What happened to opening our Bibles every chance we get to know our God deeper? What happened to just praising Him for all the small things, not just when we are going through hard times or want something?

Men, God is not our personal genie, He is a God to be reverenced. Christianity is not a casual thing. Being a man of God is not a casual thing. The world does not need any more casual Christians; it needs real men who are pursuing God with everything they have.

I remember what it was like to play Christianity. I remember a time where no matter what I did, I had an empty feeling inside me. I went to church every Sunday and Wednesday, but I felt no different from the world. For seven years I felt no change in my lifestyle. I felt so lonely.

There were times when I would drive an hour and a half to the big city and go to the mall to surround myself with people. But no matter how many people were around me, I still had an empty feeling inside of me. What was wrong with me? What was missing in my life? I was a Christian now. I went to church! I kind of read my Bible... sometimes. But why was I not changed? It was because I lacked a real relationship with God.

Let's say I was married but I never spent time with my wife. I would pass by her on occasion, moving through the house, but I never sat down to get to know her or just be in her presence. I never truly sought her out. We were married, right? But why did it not feel right? Why did we not feel married? It's because even though we were married, we did not have any fellowship. There was no real intimacy between us. This is what so many men have and where so many men are at. They call themselves Christians, but they know nothing about God. They do not have a relationship with him. That was me for 7 years of my Christian walk. What was I missing? I was missing an intimate, authentic relationship with God our Father, Jesus Christ, and the Holy Spirit. Without that encounter, my manhood was as sure as dead. I felt dead because even though Christ freed and opened the prison door for me, I was still sitting in my cell. Men, the door is open, we just have to walk through it.

This book is meant to teach you, not to condemn you. It was written to open the eyes of the spiritually blind and encourage you. It was written to show you Jesus and what

He expects of every Christian man. If this book only helps one man come to the realization of his purpose, then glory to God. I am not writing this book for the money or for the praise. I am writing this with the sole purpose of developing real godly men who want to make a difference. I am writing this to educate men on how God designed us to be. Everything we need to live a godly life has been made available to us, but we have to take the actions to pursue it. Please, take your time reading this. Read it with an open mind. If at any point you feel offended, please do not stop reading; keep going. That may be exactly what God wants you to know.

> *"These are the wise sayings of Solomon,*
> *David's son, Israel's king—*
> *Written down so we'll know how to live well and right,*
> *to understand what life means and where it's going;*
> *A manual for living,*
> *for learning what's right and just and fair;*
> *To teach the inexperienced the ropes*
> *and give our young people a grasp on reality.*
> *There's something here also for seasoned men and women,*
> *still a thing or two for the experienced to learn—*
> *Fresh wisdom to probe and penetrate,*
> *the rhymes and reasons of wise men and women.*
> *Start with God—the first step in learning is bowing down*
> *to God;*
> *only fools thumb their noses at such wisdom and*
> *learning."*
> **-Proverbs 1:1-7 (MSG)**

1

WHICH SOIL ARE YOU?

#DearChristianMen, I accepted Jesus Christ as my Savior in 6th grade. I remember asking Jesus to be my Lord and Savior while in my friend's van. His mother was the one who led me through the prayer. I felt good, but still confused by what it all truly meant. The next seven years of my life was hypocrisy and complete ignorance. Seven years passed and I still didn't know much about God, Jesus, or the Holy Spirit. I was just along for the ride; attending church every Sunday morning and Youth Group on Sunday nights. Occasionally, we would have a Wednesday night bible study for the kids. I probably entered those church doors hundreds and hundreds of times, yet never desired to truly know God. In fact, I don't even remember being challenged to dive deeper.

I would call myself a Christian, I would wear the shirts and go to the concerts and events. I would read the Bible when called upon and memorize scripture when I could. I wouldn't cuss or do any of that crazy stuff, when I was around adults at least. But honestly, if you would line my life up with those who didn't know Christ, I wouldn't be any different. Why? Because I really didn't know God at all. I called myself a follower of God, yet I didn't even follow Him. In fact, I was walking my own paths while telling everyone I was following someone. My words didn't show, my actions didn't show, and my lifestyle didn't reflect that of a true Christian in love with God.

One day in college my friend from school, Hunter, was in my business class. We started to hangout and I would take him to my place where we would play my Xbox. There was something about him that was different though. He was always so joyful and always had something good to say. He seemed so firmly rooted and confident in who he was. Whatever it was, it caught my attention. Eventually, he invited me to the bible study at his house where his dad preached. I soon realized there was so much more to Christianity than just attendance.

I will never forget the first thing Hunter's dad ever taught me. It made me really think. It made me decide what kind of Christian I wanted to be. He sat me down and opened his bible to **Mark 4** where Jesus tells a parable of the Four Soils (also in **Matthew 13:1-9** and **Luke 8:4-8**). With every word he spoke that day, purpose began to flood my life. I will never forget that moment when true Christianity started to take shape and make more sense to me. He began in verse 1.

"Again Jesus began to teach by the lake. The crowd that gathered around him was so large that he got into a boat and sat in it out on the lake, while all the people were along

*the shore at the water's edge. He taught them many things
by parables, and in his teaching said: "Listen! A farmer
went out to sow his seed. As he was scattering the seed,
some fell along the path, and the birds came and ate it up.
Some fell on rocky places, where it did not have much soil.
It sprang up quickly, because the soil was shallow. But
when the sun came up, the plants were scorched, and they
withered because they had no root. Other seed fell among
thorns, which grew up and choked the plants, so that they
did not bear grain. Still other seed fell on good soil. It came
up, grew and produced a crop, some multiplying thirty,
some sixty, some a hundred times." Then Jesus said,
"Whoever has ears to hear, let them hear."*

If you do not understand this parable, don't worry.
Jesus' disciples didn't understand it either. Jesus spoke a lot
in parables during his three and a half years of ministry.
But out of all of them, I honestly believe this is the most
important one. Why? Because without this one, we cannot
grasp or understand any other parable. **Mark 4:13** says,
*Then Jesus said to them, "Don't you understand this
parable? How then will you understand any parable?"* This
being the first thing truly taught to me, as someone hungry
for God, helped me to understand how God's whole system
works. This right here is the key to comprehend how the
Kingdom of God functions.

Jesus begins to explain it all to them in **verse 14**.
*"The farmer sows the word. Some people are like seed
along the path, where the word is sown. As soon as they
hear it, Satan comes and takes away the word that was*

sown in them. Others, like seed sown on rocky places, hear the word and at once receive it with joy. But since they have no root, they last only a short time. When trouble or persecution comes because of the word, they quickly fall away. Still others, like seed sown among thorns, hear the word; but the worries of this life, the deceitfulness of wealth and the desires for other things come in and choke the word, making it unfruitful. Others, like seed sown on good soil, hear the word, accept it, and produce a crop— some thirty, some sixty, some a hundred times what was sown."

Jesus tells us that the farmer sows the word, which makes the seed in this parable God's word. So we see here that the farmer is scattering seed (God's word) all around and onto different soils (people). Now, you and me, we are soil. We can also be the farmer, spreading the Word of God, but we are always a type of soil. When people speak the Word of God to us or when we read and learn about God and what He has done for us, seeds are spiritually being sown into our lives.

Have you ever wondered why some people receive God's Word and some don't? Or why some people seemed impacted by church and Christians, but then fall away? You wonder what happened to them or why they left. They said they liked church and they felt God move, but then they just stop coming. By the end of this chapter, I pray that you have a deeper understanding of why these things happen. I may get a little technical in this chapter, but bear with me. If you can get a hold of this, I promise it will bless you.

Gardening done grandma style

Before we dissect these soils, I want to share with you what my grandmother taught me. If you are anything like me, then you have no idea how to plant a garden. I am not going to lie, if I was given a plant, there is a good chance it will die. Seriously, do not let me house sit if you have plants. When I was younger I had the privilege of living with my grandparents. Grandparents are great, right? They are so wise and really good at cooking!

My grandma was a master gardener. For real. We had this big back yard that was just full of flowers, shrubs, trees, and a vegetable garden. It was amazing back there. I always wondered how she did it though. I was that guy that would just hire someone to do it or just go buy the plants already grown! But not my grandma. Every day she would wake up early and go out into the backyard and tend to her garden. She would nurture and care for each plant; watering it and making sure it had enough sunlight. When she planted seeds she would check the area and the soil to make sure it was good soil. If it was bad soil, she wouldn't plant it. She would make it into good soil before planting. She then would check the spacing between each plant so the plants would not choke each other off when they got bigger. She went around and pruned all the dead branches off and pulled weeds that infested the good plants. I didn't realize how much work went in to maintaining a garden. She didn't just go out and throw seeds randomly, then go back inside, and return a week later to see a full grown garden.

Men, this goes the same way with the Word of God in our lives. We can't just read a chapter out of our Bible and say, "Well, I read my chapter for the day! Done with that!" and then drop your Bible and play video games or watch TV. There will be no change in your life. There has to be meditation on the Word. We need to nurture it, water it, and tend to it. When those seeds are planted in our lives, we have a choice to make. We can either leave them to be stolen, or take care of them; protecting them from anything that can destroy or interrupt their growth. If you want to be good soil, then you must take the necessary steps to obtaining "plantable" status. Really dissect the types of soil Jesus talks about and decide what kind of soil you want to be; what kind of garden you want to look like.

Seed along the path

The first type of soil we see here is the seed scattered along the path. Jesus opens our eyes to a truth that needs to be understood. In **Luke 8:12 (NIV)** Jesus says, *"Those along the path are the ones who hear, and then the devil comes and takes away the word from their hearts, so that they may not believe and be saved."*
#DearChristianMen, we need to know this truth: Satan has the ability to steal the Word when it is sown into this type of soil. Jump over and look at Matthew's account on this soil, *"When anyone hears the message about the kingdom and does not understand it, the evil one comes and snatches away what was sown in his heart. This is the seed sown*

along the path" (**Matthew 13:19 NIV**). Men, one of the greatest dangers in the Church world today is ignorance (lacking understanding).

In **John 6**, Jesus gives a speech that would truly separate those who wanted to know Him and those who didn't. You see, Jesus was giving claims about Him being the Bread of Life and that whoever believes in Him will have everlasting life (see **John 6:41-51**). These Jews who were following him became confused. Then Jesus delivered the message that would show who His real disciples were. **John 6:53, 54** says, *"Jesus said to them, 'I tell you the truth, unless you eat the flesh of the Son of Man and drink his blood, you have no life in you. Whoever eats my flesh and drinks my blood has eternal life, and I will raise him up at the last day.'"* Sounds pretty crazy, huh? This Jesus guy was talking about eating flesh and drinking blood! And on hearing these things, many of his disciples were confused and began to complain. Many of his followers began to unfollow Him. In other words, His Facebook, Instagram, and Twitter friend count began to drop like the stocks.

Obviously, Jesus was not really talking about eating His flesh and drinking His blood. He was talking about doing so spiritually (Communion). Jesus was saying that His life had to become one with our lives. Sadly, many did not stick around to hear the rest. They didn't understand it, therefore they turned back and deserted Jesus Christ. Many of us do this today. We don't understand something and we just give up without pressing in deeper to learn more. Many pastors preach wonderful messages but as soon as you hear one mess up you throw them and all their teachings away. There is too much assuming in the Body of Christ. There are too many people acting out of ignorance and laziness. We desert the faith at the first sign of pressure. Jesus asked his twelve disciples if they wanted to leave too. They said the best answer ever, *"Lord, to whom shall we go? You have the words of eternal life. We believe and know that you are the Holy One of God* (**John 6:68, 69 NIV**)." If we claim to believe God as loving and wise, then why do we always question Him instead of responding, "You are my answer, Lord, not my problem"? The lack of understanding can cause a lot of problems and assumptions.

In the case of the seed sown along the path, we let our guard down. It's easy for Satan to steal seeds that are just lying on the surface, unprotected. In other words, the Word has to be guarded and honored so it can take root. I have seen this so many times. I guess you can say that these are the people who let the Word go in one ear and out the other. They don't take hold or honor the word. They don't take time to understand it. As the Bible says, they have "hardened" hearts. Men, we do not want to be this soil. The Word of God is not something to take lightly. If I gave you a gold coin worth millions, would you not guard it with your life? God's Word is worth far more than any amount of gold in the universe. Guard it with your life.

The seed sown on rocky places

"Others, like the seed sown on rocky places, hear the word and at once receive it with joy. But since they have no root, they last only a short time. When trouble or persecution comes because of the word, they quickly fall away." (**Mark 4: 16, 17 NIV**)

The seed sown on rocky places is the second type of soil we read here. This seed begins to grow quickly, but it doesn't last very long. Seed sown in rocky soil has no real time to develop a root system. In the end this seed has the same outcome as the first type of soil. This person heard the word and was excited about it. They received it with joy and gladness but did not take the time to let roots fully develop. To make things even worse, during times of trouble and persecution they quickly fall away (**Luke 8:13**). It's one of those truths that can be hard to grasp, but Jesus makes it very clear in this passage that persecution will come and it will come because of the Word (**Matthew 13:21; Mark 4:17**).

Men, that's going to be a given in this life. Satan is the author of persecution and affliction in our lives. It comes for the Word's sake because he wants to steal it from your heart. The number one thing Satan wants to do is steal, kill and destroy anything and everything in your Christian life (**John 10:10**). I would get used to hearing that, because we need to understand that Satan is one with no mercy. He wants to destroy any part of you at any time he can, especially seeds sown into your life. If it has anything to do with you growing closer to God, Satan wants it gone and obliterated from your life. If it's not laying on the surface to be stolen, then he wants to tear it out before it gets rooted and established. #DearChristianMen, it's much easier to pull out a baby plant than a full grown tree.

One time in 6th grade, we had a class where we all got seeds and planted a little flower. Mine finally sprouted up one day. It was only about a half an inch out of the dirt, but me not being full educated in Plants 101, was a little too rough with it and accidently pulled it straight out. Let me tell you this: it was pretty easy. It hadn't had a firm root system yet. Praise God for the mercy of some teachers, huh?

Men, we do not want to be this soil either. We want to receive the word of God with joy, but protect the seed. When the storms of this life come, and they will, we want to hold firm to God. Persecution will come on behalf of you just being a Christian. It's what happens. People will not like you, even your family may turn from you. But no matter what, we cannot be moved by that. We cannot let Satan steal the seed. We do not want to fall away. Do you want to know God more than you want to be safe?

Seed among thorns

"Still others, like seed sown among thorns, hear the word; but the worries of this life, the deceitfulness of wealth and

*the desires for other things come in and choke the word, making it unfruitful" (***Mark 4:18, 19 NIV***).*

Here the third type of soil we read about is the seed that is sown among the thorns. This soil is similar to the rocky soil because they both hear the Word of God but does not last long because of the distractions and temptations of this world. I really like how the Amplified version describes it, *"And the ones sown among the thorns are others who hear the Word; Then the cares and anxieties of the world and distractions of the age, and the pleasure and delight and false glamour and deceitfulness of riches, and the craving and passionate desire for other things creep in and choke and suffocate the Word, and it becomes fruitless"* (**Mark 4:18-19**).

The Bible warns us that there will be a time when people will be lovers of themselves, lovers of money, boastful, proud, abusive, disobedient to their parents, ungrateful, unholy, without love, unforgiving, slanderous, without self-control, brutal, not lovers of good, treacherous, rash, conceited, lovers of pleasure rather than lovers of God-- having a form of godliness but denying its power (**2 Timothy 3**). Sound familiar? This world is full of temptations to become like any of these. From the news to the schools, there are temptations to get you to worry and be distracted, to become someone you were not created to be. The peer pressure to be "popular" or the false standards of beauty that are set by so many. Without a firm root, our seeds are doomed to be uprooted and stolen.

I have seen this also so many times in my life. People who genuinely want something more in life and desire a greater purpose grab a hold of God, but not long after that, the things of this world consume them. The fear of running out becomes greater than the faith of running over. #DearChristianMen, anytime you run after God, expect the enemy to throw distractions at you. He doesn't want you to know God. He comes in many different forms. Men, do not be led astray by the things of this world. Even though those things may look better than what you have now, just know that deep down they are nothing but traps. There is no real fulfillment in them. There is no true satisfaction. I was forewarned about this before I decided to take the next step, but I wanted God more than anything. I wanted purpose, I wanted forgiveness, and I wanted to know the God who created me.

Seed on good soil

"Still other seed fell on good soil. It came up, grew and produced a crop, multiplying thirty, sixty, or even a hundred times." Then Jesus said, "He who has ears to hear, let him hear" (**Mark 4:8-9 NIV**).

The fourth type of soil we read about here is the seed that is sown on good ground. Men, this is the soil we want to be. When the seed is planted, it is nourished and taken care of. It is protected so it can develop a root system. And when the time comes it yields fruit multiplying thirty, sixty or even a hundredfold what was sown. Planting in good soil is the best investment you will ever make.

Someone once brought to my attention that the seed in good soil is just normal soil, however there is something special about it. This soil does not have more, in fact, it has less. This soil has less rocks, thorns and debris. This soil has less anxiety and less distractions, which gives it more room to grow and produce a harvest. It's not like these people don't go through trials and tribulation, but these people do not let that get in the way of them growing up in Christ. God's Word is always the same and it can work for anyone, but it all depends on the condition of the heart it is sown into.

Jesus explains a little bit more about this type of soil in **Matthew 13**, "*But the one who received the seed that fell on good soil is the man who hears the word and understands it. He produces a crop, yielding a hundred, sixty or thirty times what was sown*" (**Matthew 13:23 NIV**). When it comes to the words of God, it's not only hearing the Word that will yield a crop, but it's understanding that Word. Let's take it a step further and say that it's not enough to just *hear* the word, but *understand* it and *do* the word.

I want you to take a look at this, men. This soil is the exact opposite of the first type of soil (the seed along the path), which are those who hear and do not understand, and the seed is quickly taken from them by the enemy (**Matthew 13:19**). Understanding with action attached to it is the key to producing a harvest in the kingdom. *"Do not merely listen to the word, and so deceive yourselves. Do what it says!"* (**James 1:22 NIV**). This is where a lot of us fail. So many men listen to sermons and attend church. They go to the meetings and show up at the events. They read their devotionals and memorize some cliché Christian quotes, but there is no fruit in their life. There is no evidence. The seeds are planted because they hear what is being spoken, but they do not add the action to their learning. In other words, they are not doers, only hearers. Men everywhere are deceiving themselves because they are only hearing but not understanding. Sadly, many Christians are ok with this, as if hearing God's word will give them a free ticket into Heaven. It's not just the truth that sets us free. Many say the scripture, *"…and the truth will set you free* (**John 8:32 NIV**)," but that's not all of it, men. The previous verse says, *"If you hold to my teaching, you are really my disciples.* ***Then*** *you will know the truth, and the truth will set you free."* The truth by itself will not set you free or empower you. Only when it is accompanied by action and understanding will it set you free.

The stagnant church of Bethesda

You see men, when we become only hearers, we become stagnant. When we get a group of people together who only hear God's Word and doesn't do anything with it, we get a stagnant church, a church much like the group gathered at the Pool of Bethesda. Like me, you may have probably heard this story a hundred times but never saw it like this. This story takes place in **John 5:1-13 (NIV).**

"Some time later, Jesus went up to Jerusalem for a feast of the Jews. Now there is in Jerusalem near the Sheep Gate a pool, which in Aramaic is called Bethesda and which is surrounded by five covered colonnades. Here a great number of disabled people used to lie-the blind, the lame, the paralyzed. One who was there had been an invalid for thirty-eight years.
When Jesus saw him lying there and learned he had been in this condition for a long time, he asked him, 'Do you want to get well?' 'Sir,' the invalid replied, 'I have no one to help me into the pool when the water is stirred. While I am trying to get in, someone else goes down before me.' Then Jesus said to him, 'Get up! Pick up your mat and walk.' At once the man was cured; he picked up his mat and walked.
The day on which this took place was a Sabbath, and so the Jews said to the man who had been healed, 'It is the Sabbath; the law forbids you to carry your mat.' But he replied, 'The man who made me well said to me, 'Pick up your mat and walk,' So they asked him, 'Who is this fellow who told you to pick it up and walk?' The man who was healed had no idea who it was, for Jesus had slipped away into the crowd that was there. '"

Here we have a group of broken down people. Some are blind, some are lame, and others are paralyzed. They are all sitting by this pool called Bethesda, which is Aramaic. "Bethesda" actually means "House of Mercy." So all these people with disabilities would sit around this pool and wait for an angel of the Lord to stir the waters. When these waters were stirred, the first person in would be miraculously healed. These people were waiting for the stagnant waters to be stirred up by God. In other words, these people were waiting for a move of God. Does this sound familiar? What does this place sound like to you? We have a bunch of people who are hurt and broken and they are all sitting around waiting for a move of God. It sounds like a lot of churches now days. It sounds like a church that hears the Word but does not understand it, let alone do it. This sounds like a church that has become stagnant and lazy; waiting for God to make the first move.

But then here comes our hero, Jesus. He walks in to this "church" and asks this lame man who has been invalid for thirty-eight years, "Do you want to get well?" Wow, that's bold. Jesus just shows up, walks up to this man, and asks him the question of a lifetime, "Hey, do you want to get rid of this sickness?" Instead of saying yes, what does this man do? "*Sir, I have no one to help me into the pool when the water is stirred. While I am trying to get in, someone else goes down ahead of me,*" (see **John 5:7 NIV**) He makes a big fat excuse. Men, we do not want to be like this. We do not want to be this type of person or this type of church. There are many churches and many men out there who are sitting in their church, broken and waiting for a move of God. They are making excuses while sitting around a stagnant pool. Like many today, these people gathered regularly, hoping for God to come down and meet all their needs and make things better. In reality, you are not waiting on God, God is waiting on you. He is waiting for you to not only hear His Word, but receive it, water it, protect it, grow and mature. He is waiting for us to step out and be doers. He is waiting for us to ask for wisdom to understand what He is trying to tell us. And He is waiting for us to make the first move, a move of faith.

This man was asked a direct question, and him, not even knowing who Jesus was, was healed after being disabled and lame for thirty-eight years! Jesus told him to pick up his mat and walk, and that's exactly what he did. Can you imagine what was going through this man's mind? This man didn't even know who this Jesus fellow was. Can you imagine what could happen for a born again believer?

This man and his mat were best friends. He laid on this mat for almost forty years! This mat represented his old, stagnant lifestyle. You know what? Jesus is busting down the doors of your church and coming in and telling you, "Get up and be healed! Take your former, lazy, and stagnant lifestyle, pick it up and get it out of here! I don't want you to need that again. No more excuses. No more hypocrisy. No more staying still. You are to stand up, be healed and throw away your old life right now." That's what receiving, understanding, and doing the Word does for you. It changes everything. It brings hope and power. It changed this man. He was just hoping for a little pool to be stirred so he can get his healing. Jesus came in and gave him more. Jesus, the Living Water, came in and made his stagnant pool turn into a raging river.

Jesus finds him at the temple later on and says to him, "*See, you are well again. Stop sinning or something worse may happen to you* (**John 5:14 NIV**)." Jesus loved this man enough to correct him and direct him. I tell you this story because I love you. I do not want to see anyone become any of these bad soils, resulting in a stagnant lifestyle. I want to see you become good, fertile soil. I want to see you become men who not only hear the Word, but understand it and do the Word. I want to see you step up and become examples for others. Jesus would never have let this man go on living without warning him what sin can do. And I would never just let you guys go on without educating you on what being stagnant will get you in life. Trust me, I have been there before. I have been stagnant and I have been that Christian just sitting there, going to church, hoping for a miracle. Hoping that God would swoop down and change my life without me having to do anything. If we grab a hold of God's Word, we can go from being stagnant pools to rushing rivers of abundant life.

Good soil? I'll take t!

Hunter's father, Mark, looked at me and asked the question that would officially spark my desire to stop living in hypocrisy. "Which soil do you want to be?" It was obvious to me that I wanted to be the good soil. I wanted it so badly. I didn't want to be a hypocrite. I didn't want to live a lie. I didn't want to just play church. And I knew right then and there that I was not good soil. In fact, I am pretty sure that I was a little bit of all three soils. I was hearing the Word of God but not understanding, and if I ever did receive it with joy, the things of this world would immediately steal the seed. I was rough, rocky, and fruitless soil. I sat there in a bit of a daze but then Mark went on to explain that it's never too late to change your soil. It may not change overnight, but with diligence and perseverance, I could tend to my soil and make it into soil that would cause the seed to take root, grow strong, and produce a hundred fold harvest.

Men, as you read this book I pray that you dissect it carefully. Do not be in a hurry to get through it, but let God speak to you through these words. Do not let the seed be stolen from you. Men, it's never too late to change a lifestyle. Seriously, whatever you are struggling with or going through, there is nothing new under the sun. You are not alone.

I write this book to you not out of boastfulness, but out of humility and love. I have been through so much without God, and I have been through a lot with Him. I want you to know what I have learned so far in my short walk with Him. I am not keeping secrets, I am telling them. I am not hiding things, but bringing them out into the open. There will always be more to learn and more to write, but I am writing what I feel Him telling me to write.

How can we live a clean life? By carefully reading the map of God's word. Be single-minded in pursuit of God; do not miss the road signs that God has posted. Bank God's promises in the vault of your heart so you do not sin yourself bankrupt. Seek God for training in His wise ways of living. Delight far more in what He tells you about living than in gathering a pile of riches. Ponder every morsel of wisdom. Relish every Word of God and you will not regret it (see **Psalm 119:9-18 MSG**).

#DearChristianMen, *"Blessed is the man who does not walk in the counsel of the wicked or stand in the way of sinners or sit in the seat of mockers.* ***But his delight is in the law of the Lord, and on his law he meditates day and night. He is like a tree planted by streams of water, which yields its fruit in season and whose leaf does not wither. Whatever he does prospers"*** *-Psalm 1:1-3.*

2

MAN OF GOD

The man of God

#DearChristianMen, in the Bible, the title "Man of God," was not given to just any guy who accepted Jesus as his Lord and Savior. That title was only given to men who were sold out for God. You may be asking, "When does one earn this title?" Well, there is no *10 Step Guide to Getting Your MAN OF GOD* badge. It comes about with transformation. And it's not a title you just give yourself one day. It comes with humility, righteousness, godliness, faithfulness, love, endurance and gentleness (see **1 Timothy 6:11**). It is given when others around you see a change in you. They see outward evidence that your heart has been changed and your soul has been saved. Those you come in contact with will wonder, "Who is this guy? Why is he so different? He is not like all the other men I come in contact with." As you tell people of how God changed you and all the glory belongs to Him, the title will slowly be given to you. "Who is that guy? Oh, he is that man of God." But here is the real question: When the world looks at your life, your words and your actions, can they tell that you are a Christian? Can they tell that you are a follower of Christ? Here is a better question: if your private life was put on display, would the world still be able to tell if you were a Christian?

From the inside out

There are many who wear the name, "Christian," in this world, but there are very few of them who truly live it out. Many believe that holiness will bring acceptance, but in fact it's quite the opposite: acceptance brings holiness. If you say you are saved, then there must be outward evidence of your inward change. Let's say I was to walk into my church tonight and tell everyone, "Hey, I just got ran over by an 18-wheeler semi-truck outside! This thing was going about 85 mph and it was fully loaded!" Yet I walked to the front normally and began to preach to you. You would be asking yourself, "Who is this crazy guy?" Why? Because if I claim to have just been ran over by something that big and that fast, I would have been changed. My body would be beaten and transformed. I would have been impacted in a life changing way. I definitely would not have made it back to the church on both my legs. I would have been splattered across that whole highway. They would have probably had to peel me off the road. But this is how most Christians are. They claim to know and love God and they claim to have been impacted by His love, yet there is no change in their lives. They are still cussing, they still watch porn, they still have sex before marriage, they still judge others, and they haven't talked to anybody about Jesus in who knows how long.

If people can't tell you apart from your old self, or even the people who live for this world, then we have an issue here. I say this boldly, but know that these are the questions I ask myself every day. Am I letting Christ live through me? Are my words of love and encouragement? Am I setting my eyes on the things of God? Am I living a holy life? Can people see Jesus in my actions and in my words?

I wasn't always aware of God's calling to manhood. I remember my first eye opening experience where I realized I had so much to learn. My best friend, who actually was the one who led me to the Lord, was always trying to plan times to hang out with me. I wanted to hang out with him, but I was always the guy who just said yes without actually knowing if I could hang out. There were many times where he would text me or call me and I would surprise him with, "Oh man, I'm so sorry bro, is there any way we can do this tomorrow?" I would just cancel at the last second. You know those people who just say "yes" without really hearing the full plan? That was me. I said yes to things just to get people to leave me alone or because I didn't want to disappoint anyone. Which in the long run ended up hurting people.

One day I cancelled on him again and he gained some boldness with me and flat out said, "Bro, I am going to be honest. It's hard to rely on you. You change your mind at the last second and you make so many commitments that you become unreliable to some of them." I was shocked. Those words hit me like a ton of bricks, but it was the truth. I was unreliable and not a very faithful man. How could I become a man of God if I was not showing characteristics of my Creator? God is faithful and His yes means yes and his no means no. I should be reflecting and imitating Jesus Christ. It was my first eye opening experience as a new believer in Christ when I realized I was far from perfect and I needed some work. But you know, we all start somewhere right? It reminds me of one of my favorite people to read about in the Bible, David. David was a man who made mistakes and learned from them. When he was dying, he gave his son Solomon advice that he learned over the years to help him live a life worthy of the calling of God.

Show yourself a man

This is a story of King David (same David that killed Goliath) and his son Solomon. David is on his death bed and getting ready to pass. He wants to leave his son Solomon with the best advice he could possibly give a young boy; the best advice any young man needs to know and be taught. Let's start in **1 Kings 2:2-3**. *"I am about to go the way of all the earth,"* he said. *"So be strong, act like a man, and observe what the LORD your God requires: Walk in obedience to him, and keep his decrees and commands, his laws and regulations, as written in the Law* *of Moses. Do this so that you may prosper in all you do and wherever you go."*

#DearChristianMen, if you want to know how to be a real man, then dwell on what David said. He is giving his son the secrets to success in life. He is trying to paint Solomon a picture of what a real man of God looks like. The first thing he tells him is to **be strong** and **act like a man**. Let's really look at this. David could have said anything here. When we think about what it takes to be a man, I honestly believe obeying God would not be on our top five. That's just something we don't really think about. We would probably say something like, "Be strong, work out, and have muscles. Save up as much as you can so you can afford a nice car. Make sure you go to college and get a degree. Get married and have kids." Not that these things are bad, but these things do not make someone a man of God. I have seen men with kids and they are still childish and selfish. But like I said, these things do not make us a man, but gives us opportunities to prove ourselves as men of God.

David told Solomon the one thing in this life that gives us a 100% success rate of showing ourselves to be men of God: Obedience. But not just to anyone or anything; obedience to God. He looks at his son and tells him, **observe** what the Lord your God requires, **walk** in obedience to him, and **keep** his decrees and commands, his laws and regulations. Observe, walk and keep are the key words I want us to look at here. I believe they go hand in hand. #DearChristianMen, growing up and becoming a man after God's own heart is not rocket science. Seriously, there is no top secret formula. It's not hidden, it's not locked away, and honestly, it's not that hard. We just be… obedient.

1) **Observe, look, read, study and dwell on God's Word.** Read it in the morning when you wake up and read it before you go to bed. Really dive in to it and I promise that when you read it in search for God and answers, you will find those very two things. It's not my promises though, the Bible tells us that if we ask, it will be given to us; if we seek we will find; and if we knock, then the door will be opened to us. *"For everyone who asks receives; he who seeks finds; and to him who knocks, the door will be opened,"* (**Matthew 7: 7; 8 NIV**).

2) **Walk in God's ways.** A lot of things I am saying may sound so cliché to you; like they belong on Instagram in big fancy fonts on a nature background that has nothing to do with the words. Seriously, as I am writing this right now I am thinking in my head, "Are these words making sense? Am I really getting through to the reader? Am I really getting through to YOU. Or does this book sound just like every other book out there?" #DearChristianMen, when I was learning all this, it was overwhelming for me. I was feeling like God was asking too much from me. I felt like being a Christian was just a long list of "do's and don'ts." God wants me to walk in His ways? But isn't going to church on Sundays and maybe sometimes on Wednesdays good enough? I throw some money in the offering plate sometimes. I bow my head when I pray. I sing the songs

and I even raised my hand once! I am a good guy, I have never killed anyone or robbed a bank. Dude, trust me, I have thought all the same stuff. I thought it was enough and that maybe those things would secure me a spot in heaven. Maybe I would have still gone to heaven, but I was still searching for something. Seriously, God calls us to do more than just hear and read His Word. He calls us to do more than just hold out for Heaven. In **James 1: 22 (NIV)**, Paul tells us, *"Do not merely listen to the word, and so deceive yourselves. <u>Do what it says</u>."* We shouldn't fool ourselves into thinking that we are listeners when really, we are anything but. We tend to let the Word go in one ear and out the other. Men, act on what you hear! It's not just about you. It's about others who watch you and look to you.

Role model let down

Let me tell you a quick story. I had a friend who I really wanted to get involved with church. He was the type of guy that when he grabbed a hold of something he really went all in. He moved one day from Iowa to Texas and I heard that he started going to church down there. I was so excited! He told me that he had an awesome youth pastor. My friend looked up to this guy so much. This youth pastor sounded like an awesome dude. You know that guy (or girl) that you notice that you enjoy being around? He is funny and mature and you just really admire the way he does things. He is a respectable guy. He was that guy who knew the balance between fun and seriousness. He seemed like such an awesome example and his joy from the Lord really showed.

But one day my friend caught him smoking weed. He played it off like it was no big deal. My friend's whole world was thrown into confusion. Could this really be the same Christian man that he looked up to? My friend was confused and devastated. This man who was a role model for so many young adults was doing something that a Christian should not do. Now, before you get all technical about marijuana and drugs, you're missing the point. Yes, we are not perfect. Yes, the youth pastor is human and he can make mistakes. But the point is this: Whether you know it or not, people are watching you. Believers and non-believers. They are looking to see if you are who you proclaim to be. And if you go to church and proclaim you are a "Christian," yet live as the world does, then the world will see that. Not only will you give yourself a bad rap, but you will actually cast a shadow on Jesus Christ himself.

People will find themselves saying, "So that's Christianity? So that's what Christians do? I thought they were supposed to be set apart. Blah blah blah." Yea, I know, they are judging and they don't fully understand the whole picture, but do you blame them? A lot of people don't understand real Christianity and the full picture because men and women are not displaying the real Christianity! We have a lot of people proclaiming things and not living up to them! If I went around telling everyone I drive a Lamborghini and then show up in a 1990 Subaru Hatchback, you're gonna think, "This dude is a liar... and needs a new car!" We need to be men of our words. We need to not only listen to the Word, but do it.

3) **Keep the Word**. The third thing David tells his son Solomon is to KEEP the Word. You know, it's not hard to get on fire for God. That's actually the easy part. The hard part is staying on fire for Him. We get encouraged and hear an amazing testimony. The passion in our hearts grow and we think to ourselves, "I want to be better." It's like a New Year's Resolution. We get determined and make all these goals. We tell ourselves, "I am going to start working out more!" And for the first week we go strong. We make it to the gym every day or every night. It looks like we have really changed. But two weeks in or three weeks in we began to slow down. The desire to be lazy grows more and more. Working out is not the new and fresh thing in our lives and we get distracted by other things.

Before we know it, that New YEARS resolution turns into a new WEEK resolution and we cancel our gym membership. We try to settle and justify things. "Maybe I will just workout once a week. I am not in that bad of shape." In reality we are saying, "It's too hard. I am too lazy to do this. I do not want to work hard to achieve more. I want to settle. I want to just be comfortable." It's just like this in our Christian walk. After an awesome message we get built up and motivated. We see a Christian who actually lives their lives accordingly and we get pumped up and want to get our lives together. We make goals and tell ourselves how we are going to be better, how we are going to read our Bibles more and minister to more people, and encourage others more. Yet, after a week or so, our fire grows dim. We lose our determination to be better. We start to make excuses. Before we know it, that fire is out and we are back to our old selves. We justify our actions. We tell ourselves things like, "Maybe I am just not ready to go all out for God. I am still a pretty good person." We let our guard down and we reach a point where we are comfortable; a place where there is little to no growth. Truth is, we might as well be honest and say, "I don't really want it enough." It's easy to talk about goals and plans, but the hard part is actually meeting those goals.

Do you really want it?

#DearChristianMen, this can't be. The desire to be better must be greater than the desire to be comfortable. Don't get discouraged though, brother. Seriously, it's not easy. But don't let that be your excuse not to go all out for God. David was a man who knew how hard life was. Temptation was all around him, especially as king. He had access to so much sin. He could have anything he wanted! David even got himself in some trouble. If you recall the story, he was outside on the roof of his palace where he saw a woman bathing. He sent for her. Of course, she was a married woman, but David was so distracted by her beauty that he slept with her. Bad move, David. She became pregnant. Double bad move, David. He then brings her husband home from war to get him to go home and sleep with his wife, but he doesn't. David doesn't want to get caught so he sends him to the front lines, where he dies in battle. At the end of this story, which is in **2 Samuel 11, verse 27,** the scriptures tell us that the Lord was not pleased with what David did. David's friend, Nathan, later came to him and confronted him and David knew what he did was wrong. David repented after that and the death of his son, and started fresh with God. What I am trying to say is that David messed up big time when he was trying to live for the Lord, but he repented and God forgave him. Don't feel bad when you mess up. Don't make it more difficult than it really is. Keep trying and keep moving forward.

The fire is out

Let me finish this part up real quick. The reasons people do not stay on fire for God may be one of these: 1) They are not reading their Bibles as much as they should, 2) They have no accountability partners; friends who love God and will keep them from straying away, 3) They are not rooted in a firm church who preaches the true Word of God, or 4) They have no determination to want to be better; they are lazy. These are just four reasons but I am sure there are more. When you have these four things, your chances of **keeping** the fire are way high. You have to want it though. Do you want it? Do you really want it?

Time is valuable, and available

There are times when many men and women stepped up and wanted to become leaders and wanted to really run after God. Eventually, excuses came up. The one I heard most often was, "I just don't have time." I understand life can get pretty busy. We have to work and many people have kids and a spouse to attend to. Life can be pretty full sometimes. But I want to be honest with you. If you really want it, you will make time. Some of you may be saying, "CJ, you have no idea what my schedule is like!" You're right, I don't, but hear me out.

If any of you have ever been in love, you know exactly the truth to my statement. When we find a girl we adore, we will go out of our way to spend time with her, buy her gifts, surprise her, and even travel long distances to be with her. We will cancel time with friends and even family to be with the one you love. Even if your schedule is busy, you will try your best to squeeze in those moments with her. We tend to do that, huh? But why not towards the Creator of the Universe?

We can be so full of excuses, trying to justify our lack of commitment. Why not be honest with ourselves? If we really, truly wanted to know God better, we would sacrifice some things in our lives in order to keep the fire going. If we truly had the desire to be used by God, then we would make time to study our word, go to church, and pray. We would put down that controller or turn off the TV and instead, we would read our Bibles or listen to a sermon. That's all there is to it. There's not some deep hidden message here. You either want it, or you don't. Don't let the fire go out, men. Fight for it.

His commands are no burden

"This is love for God: to obey his commands. And his commands are not burdensome." John wrote that in **1 John 5:3 (NIV)**. I want to end this section with this: Jesus never said that denying yourself and picking up your cross would be easy. When he spoke of picking up your cross, he was basically telling everyone to pick up this instrument of death and follow him; dying to one's self every single day. He wanted those who were listening to know the cost of following Him and that it would not always be an easy road to take.

You may have to sacrifice some things in life for God. Actually, you may have to give up a lot. But the things you gain are far greater than anything you will give up. The tasks he asks of us may not always look easy and they may not always be easy, but He tells us to do His word with our best interests in mind. Keeping his commands are not burdensome, in fact, they are life giving. True success comes with obedience to God. Experiencing true life comes with obedience to the Father. When we ignore God's leadings, we are actually settling for less. You'll never know God's best unless you try it.

3

NO REGRETS

#DearChristianMen,

One day you will look back on your life and give a testimony of your journey. What do you want to be known for? When people mention your name years from now, what will they say about you? Will you have left a legacy that glorified God? Or will you have left a legacy that glorified yourself? The thing is, you do not want to look back on your life and be remembered for the foolish things you did, the time you wasted, the mistakes you made, the bad company you hung out with, and the hearts you broke; including the harm you did to both your soul and body. You do not want to regret missed opportunities. One day you will go before God and give an account for everything you did and did not do for His Kingdom (see **Revelation 20:11-15**). He will judge you based on what you did with what you were given. Sadly, for a lot of men out there, they won't be judged so much on what they did, but what they **didn't** do.

So let me ask you, are you making the most out of what you have? I know it sounds so cliché, but I honestly want you to think about this. Men, more than anything, I want you to be honest with yourselves. If you are not honest with yourselves when examining your own life, you are only cheating yourself. I do not say this to put fear in you. I say this to put hope in you; that this very moment, whatever it is you find lacking in your life, you can change that. Jesus Christ is the only thing that truly matters and with Him comes no regrets. *"The blessing of the LORD makes one rich, and he adds no sorrow with it,"* (**Proverbs 10:22 NKJV**). But with the world and its desires, there will always be regrets of some sort. And men, at the end of your race, the amount of money you obtained will not matter. The house you own will be gone forever. The car you drive will mean nothing. The job you worked will be forgotten. There will be no trophy for the amount of girls you have been with. It will all be burned away in a fervent fire. You could have read the Bible a thousand times and remembered every verse, but if you did nothing for the Kingdom of God, then all that knowledge will be worthless. A time will come when it's not going to be about what you heard, but what you did.

But my past…

Right now you may be thinking of your past and all your wrongs. They may even be playing through your mind right now. Hey, you can't change your past; it's done and over with. But you can change your future. You can repent right now and ask for forgiveness from God (if you haven't already) and He will forgive you. *"If we confess our sins, he is faithful and just and will forgive us our sins and purify us from all unrighteousness"* (**1 John 1:9**). He would forget all your sin right now and you can have peace in the moment if you let Him (see **Isaiah 43:25**). I guess I should ask the basic question: do you know what repentance is? Honestly, I didn't fully understand what repentance was for most of my walk. I messed up, I told God I was sorry and I messed up again on the same thing (purposely), then apologized again. For me, I used God's grace as a credit card to sin. Thing is, repentance is not only asking for forgiveness, but it is <u>changing your ways</u>. True repentance is from the heart. It means you truly are sorry for your mistakes and you want to make a change to be better. It's not just talk, it's action. And men, it's not just a one-time act, but a continual act of putting our flesh down and giving our entire self (Life, words, and actions) to God. Are we forgiven? Of course. Do we still make mistakes? You bet! But our relationship with God is not built on how much sin we can get away with. It's built on love and honor.

You see, when we mess up, a lot of the time our first thought is, "Man, I really disappointed God… again." Condemnation keeps us from starting fresh with God because we do not think we deserve it. In reality, God's first thought is, "I still love you! Just ask for forgiveness and we can get on our way." If we only got what we deserved then His forgiveness would be a reward, not a gift. God's grace and mercy is a beautiful gift, and it's given to you freely through Jesus. A fresh start is available right now, no matter what you have done. I say this now because condemnation will hinder you from receiving anything God has to offer you. Even worse, regret and an "I am not worthy" mindset will keep you in bondage. When we think like this we tend to turn down the free gifts of God. Almost like our sins were too much for Christ to handle. Like He didn't do enough at the cross.

Men, Jesus was the best there was. He got the job done and he died for ALL sin, yes, even your worst sin. This section is kind of a side step off the message I am trying to get at right now, but hear me out. I have been thinking about this phrase for a while now. I don't know if you're like me but I tend to overthink a lot (It's something I am working on). I take something like the Grace of God, and I make it more difficult than what it actually is. Jesus says, "Here, take my love, take my Grace, take my healing, take my peace, and take my forgiveness," and I respond, "Jesus, no, let me do work for you before you give me this. I mess up so much, I don't pray enough, I don't sing enough to you, I don't do this or that. I'm not worthy yet." Have you ever found yourself saying this? Have you ever thought like this? Have you ever paid for someone's meal and they insist on paying you back? You tell them it's ok, but they keep insisting on repaying you. You just want to yell, "JUST RECEIVE IT! IT'S A GIFT!"? It's frustrating, isn't it? I believe Jesus is like that towards us when it comes to salvation. Not that he is frustrated with us, but it must be hard for Him to have so much for us yet we turn it all down.

Like I was saying earlier, there has been a phrase that's been on my mind lately; three words that have changed my life. **"It is finished**," is the phrase I have been thinking about. Jesus said this while on the cross before He died. This phrase actually translates to *tetelestai (Greek)*. According to Blue Letter Bible, this word means, "to bring to a close, to finish, to end."[1] In other words, what Jesus came to do was completed and our debt was stamped with the three little words: "PAID IN FULL." That's what Jesus did; he purchased our freedom. He paid for our debt in full. And all he wants from us is our devotion, because He knows within His will, there is true life. Instead of fighting it and making His Grace difficult, just receive it and everything He paid for you to have. He loves you. I say this because I want to slowly allow you to remove baggage from your load. How are you supposed to pick up your cross when your hands are full of unwanted luggage?

The loaned money

I want to tell you a story. This story begins in **Matthew 25 verse 14 (NKJV)**. In this passage Jesus is speaking to his disciples and explaining to them what the Kingdom of Heaven will be like. So Jesus in response tells them this parable of the loaned money.

"For the kingdom of heaven is like a man traveling to a far country, who called his own servants and delivered his goods to them. And to one he gave five talents, to another

*two, and to another one, to each according to his own
ability; and immediately he went on a journey. Then he
who had received the five talents went and traded with
them, and made another five talents. And likewise he who
had received two gained two more also. But he who had
received one went and dug in the ground, and hid his lord's
money. After a long time the lord of those servants came
and settled accounts with them.*

*"So he who had received five talents came and
brought five other talents, saying, 'Lord, you delivered to
me five talents; look, I have gained five more talents
besides them.' His lord said to him, 'Well done, good and
faithful servant; you were faithful over a few things, I will
make you ruler over many things. Enter into the joy of your
lord.' He also who had received two talents came and said,
'Lord, you delivered to me two talents; look, I have gained
two more talents besides them.' His lord said to him, 'Well
done, good and faithful servant; you have been faithful over
a few things, I will make you ruler over many things. Enter
into the joy of your lord.'*

*"Then he who had received the one talent came and
said, 'Lord, I knew you to be a hard man, reaping where
you have not sown, and gathering where you have not
scattered seed. And I was afraid, and went and hid your
talent in the ground. Look, there you have what is yours.'
"But his lord answered and said to him, 'You wicked and
lazy servant, you knew that I reap where I have not sown,
and gather where I have not scattered seed. So you ought to
have deposited my money with the bankers, and at my*

*coming I would have received back my own with interest.
Therefore take the talent from him, and give it to him who
has ten talents.*

*'For to everyone who has, more will be given, and he will
have abundance; but from him who does not have, even
what he has will be taken away. And cast the unprofitable
servant into the outer darkness. There will be weeping and
gnashing of teeth.'*

#DearChristianMen, this parable right here is what
living for God is all about. Jesus obviously represents the
master in this parable. He has given us all talents or
responsibilities as followers of Christ. We all play a role in
the Kingdom of God here on earth. It doesn't matter if you
don't think you're good enough. It doesn't matter if you
think you're not good looking enough or athletic enough or
smart enough. Let me give you a heads up, if God only
called those who were qualified to serve, He would have
nobody.

As the Bible tells us, *"But God chose the foolish
things of the world to shame the wise; God chose the weak
things of the world to shame the strong,"* (**1 Corinthians
1:27**). In other words, God wants you. Whether you think
you can do it or not, He wants to use you. Men, God grabs
a hold of broken and worn down men of this world and He
transforms them into warriors. We may have been broken
when Christ found us, but if we let Him fix us up, we are
no longer unworthy, but royalty; warriors fit for battle.

For to everyone who has, more will be given

Let's talk about this parable real quick. From what we read we can see there were two smart and hardworking servants and one lazy servant. The two smart ones took what their master gave them and multiplied it. But as for the lazy servant, he hid away what the master gave him. Think about this, the guy only had one thing to deal with and couldn't even do that! But what's worse is the fact that his excuse was directed to a false accusation towards the master. What was his excuse? His excuse of not going out and doing anything was because his master was a thief. He accused him of reaping what he did not sow and gathering where he did not scatter seed. In other words, he saw God as someone who collected the benefits of the harvest, without actually putting in the work. The servant became fearful to expand what was given to him because he didn't want the master taking it all.

If you think about it, the servant felt as though what he earned was his own and did not belong to the master, yet his earnings would have been the masters anyway because it was the master who gave him what he had in the beginning. Think about this men, there are many men out there who do not live fully for God because of a misconception they have towards Him. It creates a fear in us that pushes us away from serving God. It makes us make stupid choices and crazy assumptions on who the Master really is and how He handles things.

My pastor told us once that many Christians try and view God and His love based on how much *they* love. In other words, we try and imagine God based on our own goodness scale and how we handle things. Instead of us made in God's image, we try to make God into our image. This produces false accusations and assumptions of God. The master in this parable gives this lazy servant no room for excuses. He gave the servant talent and expected him to at least do something with it. Even if it meant talking to someone about God's goodness. It didn't have to be some spectacular event. God just wants us to take things day by day and love on Him. He wants you to take what He gave you and expand it to the four corners of your block, your town, your city, your state, your country, and even the world. At the end of our lives, there is no excuse in the world that can get God to accept our laziness and fear. I don't know about you, but I know God is a just and faithful God. At the end of my life I want to hear, *"Well done, good and faithful servant. Enter into the joy of your Lord."* (see **Matthew 25:23 NKJV**).

Forgetting what is behind

I wanted to make this an early chapter so we can identify some extra baggage we may be carrying and lose it. We cannot become effective men of God if we have baggage full of regret. Trust me, I know what it's like to have those thoughts in the back of your mind of a mistake you made. I know you play it over and over again, and even play out ways you could have avoided it or ways you wish it would have turned out. I myself am a perfectionist. God has really been working with me on this area. With me, when something doesn't go as I planned it, I constantly think about it. Before I met Christ I would have probably worried myself to death. Let me tell you a story.

When going into my relationship with Leana, my soon-to-be-wife, I honestly wasn't as much of a gentleman as I thought. I would blurt out stupid comments without thinking and they would really hurt her. Being as insecure as I was, I became very sarcastic as I was growing up. I learned to cover up my feelings by cracking a joke, or worse, making fun of others. As I became a Christian, it was one of those bags that was difficult to get rid of. I remember one time we were hanging out with a couple friends and she made a comment to me. The comment kind of rubbed me the wrong way, but instead of being a gentleman and letting it go, of course I had to say something back, so I brought up something she did to me, right in front of our friends.

Men, that is <u>never</u> ever a good thing to do, especially in front of people. Seriously, if there is one thing you need to learn as a maturing Christian, it's the power of your words. Life and death are in the power of the tongue (see **Proverbs 18:21**). Later that night after everyone left she told me boldly to never do that again and how disrespectful that was. I felt terrible. I asked for her forgiveness and of course she forgave me, but I still had that sickening feeling in my stomach. She forgave me, but why did I still have this unsettling feeling? I kept playing the situation over and over again in my mind. I thought about how I could have avoided it and I began to think about how I can be better next time. I just wished an opportunity would rise quickly to prove myself that I wasn't that man anymore.

God had a talk with me that night about letting things go. I felt so much better, but it made me realize how dwelling on the things that you can't change anymore is a very dangerous thing to do. I understand we want to be better, but instead of dwelling on your mistakes, pray for opportunities to prove yourself. We tend to focus on the wrong things, and sometimes the hardest person to forgive is ourselves. The devil would love for you to live in your past so you are not useful in the present.

Straining towards what is ahead

Paul knew exactly what it meant to forget the past and focus on the future. In **Philippians 3:13 (NIV)**, Paul says, *"Brothers, I do not consider myself yet to have taken hold of it. But one thing I do: Forgetting what is behind and straining toward what is ahead."* If anyone had a crazy past full of mistakes, it was Paul. He persecuted and murdered Christians. Before he came in contact with Jesus himself, Paul's name was Saul.

We first see Paul at the scene of Stephen's death when he was stoned for his faith (see **Acts 7**). It says that Paul (Saul at the time) was there to give approval of his death. Back in the day, Paul made some terrible mistakes. One day on the road to Damascus, he met Jesus face to face and his whole life was flipped upside down. After that, he was on fire for God. In fact, God used Paul to write most of the New Testament. Paul's name was soon changed from Saul to Paul. Why? I believe it was to show that he really was a new man. I believed it helped him, and others, to see that Paul really was changed. Did Paul struggle with his past? I bet the enemy came against him a lot. If anyone had to forget their past, it was Paul. He knew exactly what it was like to mess up. He knew exactly how it felt to know deep down that his past was not pretty. Yet, he writes these words from his heart and through the Holy Spirit, *"Forgetting what is behind and straining towards what is ahead."* Although Paul's past was dark, he used his testimony to bring people to the Light. #DearChristianMen, I know it can be hard sometimes to really get past those thoughts, but the key is taking your focus off your failures and looking to something that is much bigger and better: Jesus Christ.

I believe Paul had to constantly remind himself who he was in Christ. Time and time again people would notice Paul and quickly ask, "Is this not the man that persecuted the church?" Many people knew him from his past and that's all. I went through the same thing. Not long after I truly gave my life to the Lord, I moved away from my small town where I went to middle school and high school in order to go back to the city to college. God completely changed me during those three years of being away. I met my fiancé and we both decided to move back to my hometown where my church was. I was a changed man, but a lot of people still remembered me for who I was. I wasn't crazy bad, but I definitely was far from perfect.

My point is, if we let ourselves be so easily moved by our past, the devil will make sure we become completely consumed by it. He will bring our past up every chance he gets. His goal is to get us so lost in our past, that we can't live in the present, affecting our future. Remember when I messed up with Leana and I kept thinking about it? I thought about it so much that I couldn't focus. I kept on messing up at work and people would ask me things and I wouldn't hear them. I was off in my own little world of condemnation. This is what the enemy loves to do. Paul was being used by God and if he would have given in to the distractions of his past, he may have missed the opportunity to be used by God Almighty in the now.

Don't paralyze yourself with overthinking of the things you do wrong. Trust me, you're going to mess up again. It happens, we are human. Each time though, try to learn and grow from it. Instead of getting frustrated and angry, take those situations and that energy and use them to sharpen you. Look forward to those trials and temptations because the testing of your faith produce perseverance (see **James 1:3**). The more you start overcoming those situations, the more mature and complete you will become and the less you will make those mistakes. Instead of your past holding you back, take your past and use it to glorify God. Use what the enemy intended for evil and glorify the Lord with it.

Not only forgiven, but forgotten

#DearChristianMen, once you ask forgiveness, God not only forgives you, but he forgets it. **Isaiah 43:25** tells us, "*I, even I, am he who blots out your transgressions, for my own sake, and remembers your sins no more.*" It's not that God has a memory problem. He knows everything; He is God. The thing is, He chooses to forget our sin when we ask for forgiveness because He loves us. That's what true love does, it does not keep record of wrongs. In our daily relationships, we can choose to remember the wrongs someone has committed against us, or we can choose to forget them. To forgive someone, we must often put those painful memories away and out of our minds. It's obvious that those memories are not just gone forever. If we really wanted to I bet we could recall the things anyone has ever done against us. The thing is, we *choose* to overlook them. Forgiveness is a beautiful thing that frees us from the bondage of a grudge. Forgiveness is actually the key to living in the now instead of the past.

So many men pray and ask for forgiveness, but it's still on our minds. Just like with Leana and me; she forgave me but I was still thinking about it. Why? She may have forgiven me but it's because I hadn't forgiven myself. Those thoughts of our bad choices may always pop up in our minds, but that is when we have to remember what Jesus did for us and the fact that God doesn't remember them. So why should we? We must cast those thoughts down or in simple words, "throw them away." The King James Version says it best in **2 Corinthians 10:5**, "*Casting* *down imaginations, and every high thing that exalteth itself against the knowledge of God, and bringing into captivity every thought to the obedience of Christ;"* In other words, any thought that comes against you that you know is not of God (condemnation), you are called to get rid of it; to not dwell on it; to make it line up with God's word.

This may sound confusing for some, but in the simplest words I can find: Do not accept the lies of the enemy that you are unforgiven or not worthy of forgiveness. We can't fight those thoughts with thoughts or we will lose. We literally have to speak out loud the Word of God. Can you talk and think of something completely different in your mind? Go ahead and try. We tried this experiment in church once. Start counting from 1 to 30 in your mind and then say your name out loud randomly. The counting in your head stopped when you spoke, didn't it? When those thoughts bombard your mind, I suggest you read your Bible out loud. It really does help. God's word is alive and powerful. Do you believe that? Do you believe that God loves you? He does, and He is waiting for you to completely give Him your worries and anxieties. Give Him your cares, let Him forget your sin, and be free from past wrongs.

Seriously, stop dwelling on your past

#DearChristianMen, there were men in the Bible that did terrible and horrible things, yet when they came to

God and asked for forgiveness He did not hold anything from their past against them.

Men, sometimes it's hard to imagine the God who created the stars and galaxies to come down as a human and die for those who hated Him. Who would do that? What king would die for mere peasants? What king would give his very best to redeem the very worse? It was because He loved us. Jesus went to the cross knowing that many would reject his sacrifice, but he endured knowing that there would also be many who would accept it and believe on Him. Jesus came down to earth not to condemn us, but He came to save us. He didn't come to bring judgment, and he surely didn't come to punish us. He came to purchase us back and give us a second chance at life. Do you want to spend the rest of this life living like you used to? Then lose the baggage, men. Stand up and confess out loud that you are forgiven and redeemed; that you are loved and renewed. Do not let anyone tell you otherwise.

Remember, men, it will not always be easy, but it will always be worth it. I'll finish this chapter with this. *"Rejoice in the Lord always. I will say it again: Rejoice! Let your gentleness be evident to all. The Lord is near. Do not be anxious about anything, but in everything, by prayer and petition, with thanksgiving, present your requests to God. And the peace of God, which transcends all understanding, will guard your hearts and your minds in Christ Jesus. Finally, brothers, whatever is <u>true</u>, whatever is <u>noble</u>, whatever is <u>right</u>, whatever is <u>pure</u>, whatever is <u>lovely</u>, whatever is <u>admirable</u>--if anything is <u>excellent</u> or*

praiseworthy—think about such things. Whatever you have learned or received or heard from me, or seen in me—put it into practice. And the God of peace will be with you." –
Philippians 4:4-8

"And the peace of God, which transcends all understanding, will guard your hearts and your minds in Christ Jesus." God's peace goes beyond all knowledge and understanding. Why? Because we will never understand it fully until we experience it. It goes past just mere knowledge and is comprehendible when we encounter it and live in it. I believe that is what it means. I believe we can live in His peace here on earth as well as in Heaven someday. That peace will guard us. That peace will keep us. Jesus gave us His peace and it's not a peace the world can give you (see **John 14:27**). It's in and only in that peace that you will be freed.

4

WE HAVE AN ENEMY

#DearChristianMen, we have an enemy. His name is the Devil, Satan, Lucifer, whatever you want to call him. I know, it sounds so weird. Sometimes when I talk about the devil to non-believers they just seem to look at me funny like I am telling a fairy tale or something. But men, even though the Bible tells us Jesus defeated hell and the grave through His death and Resurrection, does not mean the devil cannot get into your life. We have an enemy and he comes only to **steal, kill** and d**estroy** (see **John 10:10**). I am not trying to give the enemy applause, but I will say this: he is relentless. I put this section in this book because there are so many people out there who are ignorant of the devil's schemes. They are getting beat up by the enemy and his goons without even realizing it.

#DearChristianMen, I want you to be equipped and ready for the attacks of Satan. He does not play fair. He is the type to throw dust in your face. He wants to blind you from the truth. He is evil. He takes things that are good and twists it to make it look bad. He wants more than anything to confuse you about what is good and what is evil in this world. He will take true Christianity and try to distort and make it look bad in order to make people turn away from it. He will try to convince you sin is good and then condemn you for doing it. And men, he will promise you the world just like he did with Christ, just as long as you serve him. And one of the biggest things I have seen over the years is this: He will even let you go and play church and call yourself a Christian, just as long as you do not know the true power of God. Men, *"be self-controlled and alert. Your enemy the devil prowls around like a roaring lion looking for someone to devour,"* (**1 Peter 5:8**).

An angel of light

Here is where a lot of people miss it. So many Christians think Satan will come at them wearing a red suit and holding a pitchfork. No, not even close. He doesn't always attack you from the front with a big sign that reads, "I am going to tempt you!" In fact, the Bible tells us that Satan masquerades as an angel of light (see **2 Corinthians 11:14**). In other words, he dresses up as beauty in order to lure you in to sin. He will make sin look fun and completely worth it. He will take things that are ugly deep down and make it look attractive. He can make a turd look good (yes, I said turd).

#DearChristianMen, do not fall for his traps. Do not let your guard down. Do not be so easily entertained. Let's take a look around. Let's take smoking for example. You can get hooked on it. From the outside it looks fun.

You get that relaxing feeling going on and your stress just disappears for a while. Pretty good right? Satan takes something that kills and makes it look and feel good. Deep down, smoking destroys your body from the inside out. It makes your clothes smell bad, your breath smell bad, your teeth turn yellow and the inside of your body turn black. It's a cancer that was not created by good people to ease your pain, it was created by someone influenced by the enemy who wants money, even if it means destroying people to get it. This is exactly how the enemy works. **2 Corinthians 2:11** tells us that we must not be outwitted by Satan. We must be aware of his schemes. How do we do that? Read the Word of God and learn his tactics and patterns.

The double kill

I like to call this one, "The Double Kill." Why? Because the devil will tempt you to sin and make you think it's alright. He will tell you things like, "It's not that big of a deal. You could be sinning worse." Or, "Jesus will forgive you." And when you decide to give in he will turn the tables and condemn you, "You are dirty. You are a worthless sinner. You can never be a good Christian. You are not even a Christian!" He gets you twice, which is why I call it the double kill. It happens a lot and has happened plenty of times for me. He will pounce on any chance to condemn you. He wants you to feel guilty, he wants you to get mad and sad, and he wants you to give up.

Condemnation

One of his main attacks is condemnation. He doesn't want you to feel worthy. He doesn't want you to feel good about yourself. He doesn't want you to have any hope of becoming an amazing leader for God. He will show you no mercy. He wants us to feel bad for the things we have done and the things we will do. If there is one thing the enemy will ALWAYS try to do, it's remind you of your past and condemn you for it.

#DearChristianMen, your past is forgiven. Christ died for you to not only forgive your past sins, but every single sin you will commit. Does that mean we go out and sin on purpose? No. But it does mean that God is not sitting there waiting for you to sin, and when you do, He becomes extremely disappointed in you and gives up on you. Satan wants you to think God is mad at you. He wants to convince you that the life God wants you to live is too much and that we are not even worthy enough to live it.

Romans 8:1 tells us, *"Therefore, there is now no condemnation for those who are in Christ Jesus."* That means that if we are in Christ, God never condemns us for our mess-ups. He doesn't point the finger, but only reaches out His hand. He doesn't yell at you for messing up, but whispers to us, "I still love you." And He doesn't take away our salvation as punishment, but offers us more grace. If you are feeling condemned, that is the enemy and you have to know it is a lie.

It's not always the devil

As much as I hate what the enemy has done to this world, I feel like we blame him for more than we ought. I have heard many people say, "The devil made me do it." As much as the devil tempts us and hates us, he can't force you to sin. He can't force you to do anything. We always have the choice to sin or not. Some Christians use this as a cop out for a "no-fault" Christianity, where they do not have to take responsibility for their own actions. Listen up men, a lot of the time we are the ones who slip up and make a mess. We get ourselves in these terrible situations and we say things like, "Oh I hate you devil!" or something along those lines. When in reality, we are the ones that walked down that path, went to that place, said those things, and sinned those sins. Yes, the devil is evil and he wants you to mess up, but we also must mature and take responsibility.

There are some times you can blame the devil, there are some times you blame yourself, but there is never a time to blame God. *"When tempted, no one should say, "God is tempting me." For God cannot be tempted by evil, nor does he tempt anyone; but each person is tempted when they are dragged away by <u>their own</u> evil desire and enticed. Then, after desire has conceived, it gives birth to sin; and sin, when it is full-grown, gives birth to death* (**James 1:13-15**). Satan and all his fallen angels will tempt you. They will try to steal your joy, steal your faith, and destroy anything and everything they can. But here's the deal, once they throw it at you, the ball is on your court. YOU decide what you do with it. As this scripture tells us, we are tempted when we are enticed and dragged away by OUR OWN evil desires. When we choose that evil desire, it gives birth to sin, which destroys. I am saying this to get you in the right mindset. It's easy to get captivated by cliché Instagram and Facebook posts that say things like, "Everything happens for a reason." You know what? They are right, everything does happen for a reason. Most of the time our dumb choices are the reason.

Even those close to you

You probably read this section's title and was like, "Whoa, my family could be the enemy???" First of all, no, no human is the enemy. *"For our struggle is not against flesh and blood, but against the rulers, against the authorities, against the powers of this dark world and against the spiritual forces of evil in the heavenly realms,"* (**Ephesian 6:12**). The thing is, we all are weak sometimes and we make mistakes. We might as well get used to the fact that we will still sin on occasion. Hopefully you sin less and less as you get closer to Christ. But that's a whole other topic.

Like I said, we all have weak points in our lives when we are more susceptible to the enemy. It's not that we are "possessed," but it's more like we are influenced by him. Even the closest and most loving Christians can say something sometimes that is not from God. For example, say you are making a huge decision. My fiancé and I are planning a wedding right now. In the process of choosing the date, we wanted to pray about it and see what the Lord thought. We chose a date and we were pretty confident about it. Some close friends of ours would make comments that I bet seemed like loving advice to them at the time, but it only discouraged. The enemy was influencing the whole situation to try and get us discouraged or second guess what we knew to be from God. Seriously, it happens. It's not like we were mad at them, or they were doing it on purpose, we just knew what God was telling us and that was that. But the enemy will try to influence even our family members to get us to lose focus or stray off course. This is why we should always be slow to speak because we want to make sure we are not doing that to others.

#DearChristianMen, the enemy's goal is to always do to us the opposite of what God wants to do to us. Instead of encourage, the devil wants to discourage us. Instead of healing us, the devil wants us sick and destroyed. Instead of prospering us, he wants us to be broke spiritually and physically. Instead of having faith, the devil wants us to be in fear. Instead of trusting in God, he wants us to doubt. Instead of being confident in who we are in Christ, Satan wants us to be insecure. He wants to confuse us, make us get angry, cause us to stumble, and keep us down. This is why it's so important to get to know God, because the more you know Him, the more you know what's not from God and what is from the enemy.

I know, I may be throwing a lot at you, but do not over think any of this. Just take it in a little bit at a time.

God is good and Satan is bad. Pretty simple, right? We need to know what to accept and what to rebuke.

What can sin do and why does God hate it?

Sin... It is evil. The only thing sin does is destroy. It may seem fun, it may seem ok, it may even seem full of life sometimes, but the Bible makes it very clear that sin is evil. It is what separates God from his creation. It's what destroyed God's original plan. It is an acid that erodes whatever it touches. All through the Bible you see God's attitude toward sin. The way He describes sin is evident enough on how much God is disgusted with it. For example, in **2 Corinthians 7:1 (NKJV)** and **Titus 1:15 (NKJV)**, sin is labeled as filthy and defiling. In **Isaiah 1:6 (NKJV)** sin is described as putrefying sores. Nasty right? **Psalm 38:4 (NKJV)** tells us that sin is a burden that is too heavy to carry. Sin is darkness that leads us away from fellowship with God. It's a dirt stain on a brand new shirt. Why does God hate sin so much? Because it's the very opposite of who He is. It's the opposite of His nature. God builds up and gives life. Sin tears down and causes death. **Psalm 5:4 (NKJV)** tells us, *"For you are not a God who takes pleasure in wickedness, nor shall evil dwell with you."*

God hates sin because He is a holy God; holiness is His number one attribute (see **Isaiah 6:3**). We are called to be holy like He is (see **1 Peter 1:16**) and when we sin we are not displaying his holiness. For those of you who are parents, you do not like when your kids rebel, do you? When they rebel, you know it's not their true nature. It upsets you and saddens you. You know their potential to live holy and right. I believe it's the same with God. When we sin, we rebel and it saddens God. He hates sin because it distorts His creation into something they were not created to be.

#DearChristianMen, God hates sin because it is everything He is not. Yes, God knows we will sin. And he doesn't hate us, but He does look for those who have a pure heart. Are you sinning on purpose? Are you abusing God's grace? Where is your heart, men?

God is better

There so much more I could write about sin and how it affects us, but I want to end on this. I called this section, "God is Better." I remember hearing a sermon by Francis Chan talking about the temptation to sin and choosing it over God. It opened my eyes to not only to the problem with sin, but it opened my eyes to how much God loves me.

Jeremiah 2 opens up in a time where God's people were really falling away. God had so much mercy on them and had done so much for them, yet they continued to turn away. **Verse 1** says, "*I remember the devotion of your youth, how as a bride you loved me and followed me through the desert, through a land not sown.*" So this is

God speaking here to Israel. This is God proclaiming His love for His chosen people. He is bringing up memories of when they were devoted to Him.

You know, for many people in this world, we think of God up there in heaven as this puppeteer pulling all the strings. We see Him as someone who constantly judges us and controls everything. Many of us may have even thought of Him as this God who kills children and gives people cancer to teach them lessons. I can bet at times in your lives you even got mad at God and maybe even considered Him a tyrant. Maybe even at times you thought you could run things better. You might even have thought God hated you and didn't even care. But this is God speaking to His people, to us. This is God speaking to YOU.

Listen to the words he uses. God is speaking to His people and he says, "I remember how devoted you were to me. How you loved me. How you followed me." Then God drops a bomb in **Jeremiah 2:5** saying, *"This is what the LORD says: What fault did your fathers find in me that they strayed so far from me? They followed worthless idols and became worthless themselves."* Wow, doesn't that sound like so many of our lives at times? We heard an awesome message, or someone came and encouraged us and we encountered God and He made things so wonderful and so beautiful, but then we just walked away towards something else. Something else pulled us away and grabbed our attention more than our loving God. We follow things that are meaningless and our plans and purpose become meaningless themselves. I can imagine God is left there saying, "What did I do? Was I not perfect to them? Did I not give you my Son? Did I not love you?"

Go down to **verse 13**. *"My people have committed two sins: they forsaken me, the spring of living water, and have dug their own cisterns, broken cisterns that cannot hold water."* Francis Chan said it best, "The people committed two sins, one was they chose their sin, but what I really think broke the heart of God was that they chose their sin over Him."[2] Wow, talk about convicting, huh? I love the boldness of Francis Chan. I love his transparency. How many times have we chosen the things of this world over God? I know I have done that plenty of times, especially back in the day. I still find myself doing it sometimes. This is what His chosen people were doing to Him over and over again. Can you believe us? We left God, the Spring of Living Water, because we thought we could build something better? We thought we could run things better than God?

The Israelites thought they could dig a hole big enough and then fill it with water, thinking it would be a better supply than what God Almighty could do for them. Men, get this, they thought that they could live and do things perfectly fine, and even better, without Him. For real? And to top it off it was a broken cistern! It wasn't even going to hold water in the first place! They were trying to fill a broken cistern with water, thinking it would do a better job than God. That's like rejecting money and instead going outside and finding dog poop and trying to pay for groceries with it. No grocery store on planet earth would accept that. It would never work. That dog poop will never replace money (This is honestly the first thing that popped in my head. Maybe this isn't the best comparison). This is what sin does to us. It draws us away from God. It draws us away from having a true and intimate relationship with Him. Sin draws us away from something amazing for something counterfeit; something not even close to the real deal.

#DearChristianMen, God doesn't give us commands because He is a slave driver. He gives us the Bible, He gives us scripture, and He gives us His law because He knows it's the best way. He knows that if you follow His Word then you will live! His commands are not burdensome. They protect and they give life. When we choose sin and to live life according to the world's way, we are choosing death, thinking it's life, and God is sitting there with a broken heart because all He wanted to do was be close to you, love you, lead you, and give you a life truly worth living.

This is the point I wanted to truly get across in this section. The enemy will always try to present this false lifestyle before you. It looks good, it feels good, and the world may even tell you that it's true living, but let me tell you this: God is better. His ways give you true life. I know people who lived "the life." My fiancé knew what it meant to truly live by the world's standards. Some could even say she was living the dream, but she can vouch for this: When she found God and started living for Him, she felt more alive than she ever has.

I know many people who turned to God and experienced things His way, and they say they would never turn back. I guess you can say it's a high that never goes away. As for me, I never partied and drank, but I struggled with much more internal things. I would be in the most crowded areas yet still feel so alone. Satan had me. But when I found God, He gave me a peace that surpassed all understanding. It was the best decision of my life, and it could be yours too. #DearChristianMen, I'm not just talking about saying a prayer and then attending church every Sunday. I am talking about truly selling out to God; running with Him and never looking back. It's true that following God will cost us much, but what many people don't understand is that not following Him will cost us so much more.

#DearChristianMen

5

LUST AND PORNOGRAPHY

Lust... Pornography... Sexual immorality... Sex... Masturbation. These are topics that a lot of churches fail to talk about to their members, especially their young ones. You're probably thinking, why can't we talk about things that are actually a concern like money or giving to the homeless? What about the widows, CJ??? I understand this is not an easy subject to write about. It's even hard for me to find the right words to say, but it must be said. The world needs to not only *know,* but to *understand* the impact pornography and masturbation has made in the Body of Christ and in the world. #DearChristianMen, you need to know that pornography is of the devil, and if it is of him then it only <u>steals,</u> <u>kills</u> and <u>destroys</u> from your life (see **John 10:10**).

For those of you that don't know, lust and pornography are HUGE problems among the body of Christ. I didn't include this area under the "We Have an Enemy" chapter because I wanted to talk about this separately. I am really praying and trying to take my time on this chapter because there is so much here that needs to be said. So please, take your time reading this. Study the scriptures, pray about it, and carefully evaluate your life. Before we really get started I just want you to know that if you really struggle with this area, you are not alone. This is an area we all struggle or struggled in. You are a soldier in an army and even though we are fighting different battles, we are all fighting in the same war.

Sin is sin

Many times we look at pornography as a minimal sin due to the fact that we are only looking and not touching. We think that as long as we are not actually having sex we are perfectly fine. Men, God views the spiritual sin just as deadly as the physical sin. Trust me, I had this wrong mindset for most of my Christian walk. I thought that as long as I didn't have sex, I was fine. I have never had sex before. Yes, I am twenty-six years old and I am getting married soon and I have never physically had sex with a woman. Some people do not believe me, while others think it's weird. Some of you may be congratulating me right now, but don't.

Let me explain. I may not have physically had sex, but I have failed in the spiritual side of things plenty of times. I have lusted when I know I shouldn't have. And as hard as it is to admit that, I want to be completely transparent with you. I deserve no award on the sexual purity side of things. Yes, I have been forgiven and made new; I am reconciled back to the Lord and washed clean by the blood of Jesus, but I say this because I want you to understand that no one is holier than anyone else because they stayed a "virgin." I am not knocking anyone out there who has stayed pure, that is awesome! Praise God. But just hear me out. If you have a Bible, turn to **Matthew 5:27** with me. **Verse 27** and **28** says, *"You have heard that it said to those of old, 'You shall not commit adultery.' But I say to you that whoever **looks** at a woman to lust for her **has already committed adultery with her in his heart.**"* Do you see this, men? I may not have physically committed adultery, but I did something that was just as bad; I lusted for those women and therefore I sinned.

You might have just realized you fall in to this category. If so, it's ok, you're not alone. I went to church for 7 years and hardly changed my lifestyle. I would go to church and look at porn all in the same day. I would sing the songs about how much we adore Him, but as soon as I left those walls I had girls on the mind. In fact, a lot of the time my friends and I would go to youth events to meet girls. We would be at church rating women on a scale of 1 to 10. There would be new girls coming into our youth group and instead of thinking, "I wonder how much she loves Jesus," it was, "I wonder who can get her to like them first." We were so young and so ignorant. I can confidently say that I am no longer that man. By the grace of God He has strengthened me to make that lifestyle no longer desirable.

As I go into my marriage, my past may not have been perfect, but with God I am not defined by my past. In fact, your past shouldn't make you weaker, it should make you stronger knowing how much God has truly saved you from. As of right now, know this: pornography is an addiction like anything else. It may seem like it is bigger than what it really is, but God is greater than any addiction or burden in our lives. The enemy is a small creature that casts a very large shadow, but in the light his real self is shown. And compared to Christ, the devil is nothing. Amen?

I could unload a bunch of pornography statistics on you, but would that really help? It's common knowledge of how many people actually look at pornography. What we need to know is not how many people look at it, but what actually makes it so bad? For me, I do not need to know any of these statistics in order to believe porn is bad. I see the effects of lust and sexual immorality everywhere I go nowadays. I hear men and women talk with such filth in their mouths, and if there is one thing that makes me upset it's how men talk about women (women do it to men too). They treat them like objects and defile them with their words. You want to know how I can tell what's in their heart? Because the Bible tells me that, *"Out of the overflow of the heart, the mouth speaks,"* (see **Luke 6:45**).

When men are talking about women in a disrespectful way, I can tell that those words are flowing from a disrespectful heart. Men, you need to ask yourself: Are my words of God? Am I talking about women in a respectful way? Do I talk about women with my guy friends as if they are some piece of meat? If you answered yes to any of these, that means you have a heart issue. And if we are honest with ourselves, it is probably a result of filling our hearts with sexually immoral things, such as pornography, sexually graphic movies, or even certain music.

As a man, I know exactly how easy it is for something to trigger an image in your mind. You could be on Facebook and see a picture of a woman and bam, you are automatically envisioning certain images. You could be driving and see a Victoria's Secret billboard and there goes your imagination. Without self-control, it's easy for the eyes to wander. Trust me men, I have been there. Pornography obstructed my view of women and how I should look at them for so long. I only saw what they could give me and how they could fulfill my desires. Their feelings and their emotional stability was not my first thought. If you dig deep down to the core of it all, it's a spirit of selfishness; complete selfishness.

Male talk

I work in a place filled with men. Every day I hear men talk about women and sports non-stop. They may say, "I am not religious," but I think in my mind, "Yes, yes you are! You talk about sports and women religiously! You make sure you watch every game of your sports team, you talk about women more than you work, and you are passionate about both beyond measure." You see, there are actually a lot of religious people in the world, just not all of them are in the right religion. Some of the men I work with talk about women as though they are either trophies or diseases. They brag about who they have seen and who they were with, and then they trash on those who did them wrong. Dating is just a game to many, and pornography and masturbation is just a way of life.

#DearChristianMen, these guys who do this are not men at all; they are males, boys, and wanna-be men. They live to only gratify the flesh. Real men do not lust after women one second and disrespect them another. Real men do not give in to water cooler talk (gossip). And real men do not put anything else above God. But do I expect anything more out of them? Not at all. They do not know Christ. All they know is that lifestyle. As for those who are saved, I do expect more out of them. If you are saved and reading this, I expect more out of you. In fact, I expect more out of myself. There will always be room for more improvement in these areas. But men, if you are part of these "Male Talks," please, get out of them. They will only pull you farther away from God and farther away from His plans He has for you.

I have seen plenty of men who are so easily influenced get pulled down the wrong path. They want to fit in, they don't want to be made fun of. They want to be a man and real men talk about those things, right? Compared to God's approval and opinion, nobody else's matters. There may be some resistance if you oppose their way of living, but who cares what they think of you? Many will become offended because of the truth. When you do things right for God, there will always be guys making fun of you. We are not here to please them; we are here to please God. We are here to speak the truth. We are called to live according to God's standards, not men's.

Pornography the drug

I heard a story from a pastor who was extremely addicted to pornography before he got saved. He said that he watched it so much that when he wasn't watching it, that's all he would think about. When he would try and quit, he would throw his DVDs away and burn his magazines, but he would eventually dig back through the trash and see what he could salvage. He couldn't stop thinking or dreaming about it. His urges grew to wanting more.

#DearChristianMen, just like any other addiction, your drive for more and more will never be satisfied. Men, lust is never satisfied. It always wants more! Just like drugs, you look around to find better videos and better pictures; you search more and more websites, getting deeper into the internet. Your flesh craves more, and you search but it's not there. You begin to think about it at school and at work, and you even think about it at church. Those images pop in your head when you close your eyes to pray, and you can barely even stare at a girl without thinking impure thoughts. You then feel like a hypocrite, sending you deeper down the road of secrecy.

Men, I just want you to know, you do not have to shout your sin to the world, but confession is powerful. When I openly discuss my struggles to my best brother in Christ, I feel a weight lifted off my shoulders. But even better, when I confess my sins to Jesus Christ, I feel peace, knowing He still loves me and has forgiven me. The thing is, so many men try to hide it and put on this front to convince everyone around them that they have it all together. There is no fooling God. If your plan is to satisfy the flesh, then it's never going to work. It will always be craving more. And if you plan on defeating it by your own strength, then you are only fooling yourself. Some of us have to quit lying to ourselves. Pornography is not ok. Masturbation cannot be justified. And admitting that you need help is your first step. It is not something you can be delivered of by hoping it just goes away. Let's get real here, men.

If you do not master this, then it will master you. Like I said, you may be able to fool everyone around you that you have it all together, but truth is: you can never fool God. I may get pretty bold, but it's because I know what it's like to be drowning in lust, but I also know what it's like to be victorious through Christ. I care for you, brothers.

Lust: the kingdom destroyer

All throughout scripture, we see sexual sin destroy so many men and kingdoms. It turned men's hearts from God and destroyed families. It caused bad reputations and had terrible consequences. Look around us; men everywhere have fallen because of their sexual sins. If you have ever read the news or watched TV, you know that men everywhere have fallen into the trap. From Doctors and presidents to teachers and congressman. Yes, even preachers have struggled with sexual sin, and it's sad how many of them have lost the battle. I don't think we realize how many men out there show strength when all eyes are on them, but living a lie behind the scenes. We have all watched as men's secrets were brought into the light for the world to see. Everything they worked for was lost. The respect they gained from those around them, gone in the blink of an eye.

#DearChristianMen, do you really want this to be your story? I am not exempt from these struggles. The temptation will always be there. Preachers and teachers of the word everywhere can fall into this. Paul knew what he was talking about when he told us that our battle is not with flesh and blood (see **Ephesians 6:12**), but with the dark powers of this world. God knew that man's biggest battle was going to be self. He knew that men would struggle within. David's battle with lust is the same exact battle we have today. Is it not true? Are not so many daily battles fought within our hearts? Within our minds? It is a spiritual fight that needs to be fought with spiritual weapons.

Beware the adulterous woman

There is a reason why Solomon, one of the wisest men to ever live, warned us about the "adulterous woman," so much.

"My son, keep my words and store up my commands within you. Keep my commands and you will live; guard my teachings as the apple of your eye. Bind them on your fingers; write them on the tablet of your heart.

Say to wisdom, "You are my sister," and to insight, "You are my relative." They will keep you from the adulterous <u>woman</u>, from the <u>wayward woman</u> with her seductive words. At the window of my house I looked down through the lattice. I saw among the simple, I noticed among the young men, a youth who had no sense. He was going down the street near her corner, walking along in the direction of her house at twilight, as the day was fading, as the dark of night set in.

Then out came a woman to meet him, dressed like a prostitute and with crafty intent. (She is unruly and defiant, her feet never stay at home; now in the street, now in the squares, at every corner she lurks.) She took hold of him and kissed him and with a brazen face she said: "Today I fulfilled my vows, and I have food from my fellowship offering at home. So I came out to meet you; I looked for you and have found you! I have covered my bed with colored linens from Egypt. I have perfumed my bed with myrrh, aloes and cinnamon. Come, let's drink deeply of love till morning; let's enjoy ourselves with love! My husband is not at home; he has gone on a long journey. He took his purse filled with money and will not be home till full moon."

With persuasive words she led him astray; she seduced him with her smooth talk. All at once he followed her like an ox going to the slaughter, like a deer stepping into a noose till an arrow pierces his liver, like a bird darting into a snare, little knowing it will cost him his life.

Now then, my sons, listen to me; pay attention to what I say. Do not let your heart turn to her ways or stray into her paths. Many are the victims she has brought down; her slain are a mighty throng. Her house is a highway to the grave, leading down to the chambers of death." **(Proverbs 7)**

Men, this is not knocking on women. There are adulterous men out there as well, but Solomon was a man of great wisdom and knew what the downfall of men could be if not careful. I myself know what this temptation is like.

Before I met Leana, I was tempted to go down this path. This woman, she knows how to get what she wants. Her words are smooth and seductive. She is attractive from the outside but inside she is only troubled. You can get blinded by her "beauty." She is irrepressible, showing defiance. She is good at what she does. I will admit, I was being blinded. This girl hung out with my basketball buddies, so I saw her often. I still knew deep down that something was not right. We were talking one night and she asked me a question, "Are you a virgin?" Feeling uncomfortable I answered, "Ummm... yes I am." She then said something that pierced my heart. "I want to take your virginity."

My heart clinched up and I was struck with a chill down my spine and arms. She was a woman who always got what she wanted. Men liked her and always wanted to be with her. She looked at me with confidence, as though I was just another man. At that point I had a choice to make. I can't explain it, but I felt weak up until that point. When she said that, the Holy Spirit and all my strength kicked in. I felt like I snapped out of a trance at that very moment.

Her words played back in my mind and my eyes were opened. What was I doing? Why did I even let myself get in this predicament? I should have ran a long time ago! I should have never even glanced down this path. I looked at her and said, "It's not yours to take." She had a confused look of defeat on her face. I walked away and never saw her again. I cried that night. It was tears of disappointment that I even let myself get that far into temptation, but it was more tears of joy knowing I didn't give into it.

Just like the man in the Proverb, I was close to being lured into her trap. I felt like I was outside her house and she was trying to get me to come in, but I felt like God grabbed me and pulled me out. My old self, being ruled by my flesh, would have taken the opportunity. And maybe most of you reading would have done the same, being led by your head instead of your heart. "CJ, it's just sex." No, it's not just sex. That's what we don't understand. Solomon made it clear it was more than just sex. I would have fallen into this trap, "not knowing it will cost me my life." It sounds extreme, but Solomon is trying to get it through our head that the choices we make in a situation like this will change things. There is a deeper understanding there. He describes it like, *"an ox going to the slaughter, like a deer stepping into a noose till an arrow pierces his liver, like a bird darting into a snare."* It is something not to take lightly, men.

That area in my life was special to me, and I wanted to give that to someone special: my wife. She meant what she said, that she wanted to "take" something that didn't belong to her. But if I would have given in, she wouldn't have had to take anything, I would have handed it over to her freely.

Men, and even women reading this, there are things that no one deserves except our husband/wife. Make those things special to you. Make it a treasure. I have made plenty of mistakes in my past when it came to pornography, lust, and sexual immorality. But at that point in my life, I made a choice, making my purity more important than my fleshy desires. I wanted to honor God with my body. I wanted to honor my future wife. I knew that someday I was going to tell my story and I wanted it to be a victorious story that glorified God. Men, do not give up. Do not give in. Do not give out.

You're not alone

#DearChristianMen, if you struggle with sexual sin, you are not alone. Whether they admit it or not, a lot of Christian men struggle with this area. **1 Corinthians 10:13** explains that there is no temptation that has overtaken you that is not common to man. Men, there is nothing new under the sun. The enemy has been tempting men and women sexually since the beginning. And yes, women struggle with lust and pornography just like men. Statistics say that men are more into it than women, but that doesn't matter, the temptation is there and it knocks on everyone's door sometime in their life. Let me encourage you for a second: being tempted does not mean you are weak or sinning. No, God warns us temptation will come. What truly matters is your reaction to that temptation. Will you give in? Or will you fight the temptation and overcome? You are not alone, brother.

How can I overcome this?

"For where your treasure is, there your heart will be also." Matthew and Luke both wrote that in their gospel (**Matthew 6:21; Luke 12:34**). The very next verse in Matthew goes into saying, *"The eye is the lamp of the body. If your eyes are healthy, your whole body will be full of light. But if your eyes are unhealthy, your whole body will be full of darkness. If then the light within you is darkness, how great is that darkness!"* (**Matthew 6:22, 23**).

We have to remember that Jesus Himself is saying this. He sees a broken people before him who seek healing and restoration. He is trying to get their focus off the things that destroy in this world and get them onto the one thing that truly gives life, Jesus. If we continue to watch and meditate on the things that are spiritually unhealthy for us, then our whole body will be infested with the disease of sin. Christ redeemed us from sin, but we have to make the choice to choose that freedom. If you roll around in mud you're going to get muddy. That's just it. So many men roll around in dirt and wonder why they are dirty. They wonder why they can't fully serve God and it's because of what they are letting in. Their treasure is not on the right place. Good eyes, good body. Bad eyes, bad body.

Jesus addressed this issue towards the Pharisees as well. In **Matthew 23:26** Jesus says, *"Blind Pharisee! First clean the inside of the cup and dish, and then the outside also will be clean."* Just because the cup looks clean on the outside doesn't mean it's clean on the inside. We have to return our focus to God. We must fight and become men of discipline. Instead of turning to the TV or computer when you're bored, turn to your Bible or turn to prayer. The deeper you get into His word and develop a relationship with God, the easier it will be to say "no" to worldly desires and "yes" to the things of God.

#DearChristianMen, do not feed yourself the lies that pornography and masturbation is ok. It's not! If you accept this sin then you will start to accept other sin and justify it. If you continue down this road, it will be all downhill from here. If you choose God every time, you will never be disappointed. Take it from someone who has seen and experienced the other side. Freedom from the addiction of lust is an amazing thing. It's a feeling God not only wants you to experience once in a while, but to live in that constant freedom.

6

GOD LOVES YOU

"God loves you" is probably a phrase you have heard many times. Sometimes it is said out of pure honesty and love, yet other times it is an empty phrase, overlooked out of repetitiveness. Some say it to unbelievers as a sign that says, "Hey, I am just saying this to look like I care." Others say it to believers as a "hey, I am thinking of you and comforting you" gesture. But there are a lot of Christians who say it from the heart. They truly mean it and believe it and want you to know that truth. God does love you. He really does. He loves us more than we can comprehend. He loves us more than we can fathom. Sometimes it's hard to believe. Sometimes it's hard to see it. But it's truth and it will never change whether you believe it or not. He will never love you any less and He can't love you anymore because He already loves you as much as someone can love.

As **1 John 4:8** tells us, *"God is love."* He not only loves us, He IS love. And if there is one truth I have learned from the Word of God, it's this: The way you see God and how much you think He loves you will determine your whole life's course.

One of the greatest failures in the Church today is not knowing how much God adores you. #DearChristianMen, your understanding of God's love will determine the success of your ministry in this life. And your ministry is not just a church ministry. Your family is your ministry, your wife is your ministry, your work is your ministry, and your kids are your ministry. How you process God's love will ultimately show in your life.

For example, if you always see God as this big guy in the sky who will maybe give you cancer one day to show you something or decide to randomly kill someone to save someone else, then your ministry will reflect that. If you don't think God loves you that much, then you will live that out. You will preach that. If you believe God doesn't heal, then you will preach that God doesn't heal, and if you preach God doesn't heal then I guarantee that you will not see the healing manifestations of God in your life. You see what I am getting at?

On the other hand, if you believe God loves you beyond understanding and believe God is a healer and not out to get you, then you will preach that. And if you preach God is a healer, then I guarantee that you will see His healing power manifest and transform in your life. #DearChristianMen, the more you learn and experience God's love in your life, the better you can love those around you. God's love is the foundation of the universe. His love for his creation is the reason why He sent his son

Jesus Christ to die for us. The whole entire Bible is a big love letter to us! And He doesn't love us because we loved Him first. In fact, **1 John 4:19** says that *"We love because He first loved us."* The only reason we can love is because of Him.

Honestly, this chapter could go on forever. There is so much to write about God's love. Obviously I want to talk about Jesus. I mean, He is the Word of God made flesh (see **John 1:14**). He is the manifestation of God in human form. I know that sounds weird for some of you, but God came down and took on a human suit in order to live a life we could never live and to die a death that we deserved; to take the wrath that belonged to us. He was raised from the dead three days later and ascended into heaven to sit at the right hand of God as our High Priest and Savior (see **Romans 8:34**). He gave us a life we didn't deserve and brought us out of death and into life. We could talk about Jesus forever, but there are certain points I want to hit that I feel God showed me.

Go, sin no more

After all this I pray you feel a touch from God and choose to better yourself. You may be thinking, "CJ, it's a lot harder than that. You don't understand what I must do. You don't understand what I have to give up. You don't understand how hard it is to change." Have you ever thought that we overthink too many things?

We, as humans, like to make things more difficult than they really are. We tend to have so much more faith in our problems then we do with the one who can save us with just the power in His little pinky finger. I think we underestimate the power of LOVE. I think we hear about love and are taught about love and read about love, but we never truly experience love because we have never truly experienced God's love, who is love. We look at a command like, "Go and sin no more," and the first thing we think is IMPOSSIBLE.

In **John 8,** there is a story told about a woman caught in adultery. Jesus sat down to teach a group of people when the Pharisees brought in a woman that was caught in adultery. They made her stand before the group and confronted Jesus saying in **John 8:4**, "*Teacher, this woman was caught in the act of adultery. In the Law of Moses commanded us to stone such women. Now what do you say?*" These men were trying to trap Jesus but he bent over and began to write on the ground with his finger. They kept on questioning him and then he finally responded with this: "*Let anyone of you who is without sin be the first to throw a stone at her,*" (see **John 8:7**). The Pharisees began to walk away one at a time, the older ones first, until only Jesus was left, with the woman still standing there. "When *Jesus had raised himself up and saw no one but the woman, he said to her, 'Woman, where are those accusers of yours? Has no one condemned you?' She said, 'no one, Lord.' And Jesus said to her,. 'Neither do I condemn you; go and sin no more,'* (**John 8:10, 11 NKJV**).

You may be thinking, "What!? What do you mean, 'Go and sin no more,'!? How does she do that? Jesus, you didn't give her any instructions or advice. You just told her to go and stop sinning!" Hard command, huh? But I believe it was much easier than we think. This woman just encountered grace himself. She was shown the greatest act of love: forgiveness and mercy. She felt his love, she experienced his love. She was saved by the Master. Her sin was exposed for the world to see and Jesus told her, *"Neither do I condemn you."* She was impacted by the Author of Love, which I believe made it easier for her to actually leave from there and lose her lifestyle of sin. She met perfection. Was she going to sin again? Probably. But she encountered redemption and her life was changed forever. She was given an opportunity to start fresh.

Many people see Christianity as this command. They see it as a life impossible to live so why live it, right? How can anyone go and leave their life of sin? Not many realize that it becomes a reality when you have a true encounter with Jesus Christ. His love changes things. #DearChristianMen, your life can change with one word from God; one word from LOVE. Jesus constantly presents the opportunity to a fresh life. Why? Because He loves you and He wants you to have that life.

The God kind of love

One of my favorite examples of God's great mercy and love for us is in Hosea. It is a story of a man of God,

Hosea, who was told by God to marry this woman by the name of Gomer. Thing was, she was a prostitute. I know what you're thinking, "Why would God do that to Hosea?" It's insane, I know, but I believe it was to show the world at the time and the world to come of how great God's love for us is.

If you think about it, we were like prostitutes at one point in our life. And yet God still chose to love us. In our society today, if someone doesn't love you, you leave and give up on that person. You seek to find what's lovely because it's easier. Maybe not everyone does that, but the majority of people in this world are raised to love things that love them, and once that thing or person stops loving you the way you want them to, you need to move on. But if that was real love, God would have stopped loving us a long time ago.

What if love was something beyond that? What if true love was so mind boggling, so far out there, and so scandalous, that we couldn't even begin to reach the depths of it? What if love went deeper than emotions? All the scriptures of love can be pieced together to show us a picture of what real love is. Real love is unconditional love. God's love for us is unconditional. In other words, His love for us does not change based on condition. He loves us when we mess up, He loves us when we are doing right. This love is the God kind of love. This is the love we should display to others around us, especially our spouses.

When someone doesn't love you back or love you

the way you want to be loved, we still love them. Why? Because our love is not influenced by situation or condition. It sounds crazy, doesn't it? But it's real and it's powerful. God's love for us is something that needs to be understood, or at least somewhat grasped. And I believe that the story of Hosea and Gomer is an awesome example of God's never ending mercy and grace. I am going to start off in Hosea 3 where Gomer has left Hosea and their three kids and God tells Hosea to go find his wife.

Go find her

Maybe one of the best stories of redemption in the Bible is Hosea and Gomer. Although this chapter is only 5 verses long, it displays such a beautiful picture of how much God loves His children. **Hosea** Chapter **3:1** starts off by saying, *"The LORD said to me, 'Go, show your love to your wife again, though she is loved by another man and is an adulteress.'"* First scripture in and you are probably already like, wait WHAT? Now, if you don't know the story, Hosea was a man of God who was tasked to do something unthinkable. At a time when God's people were lost and worshipping other gods, God told Hosea to marry a prostitute by the name of Gomer. It was to show the world exactly what God's relationship to the Israelites were like at the time. It was to show how much God loved his people, even during their darkest moments. It's overwhelming if you really think about it, but Hosea obeyed the Lord anyway.

They married and had three kids. But this story doesn't end like that. Gomer got pulled back into her old lifestyle and abandoned Hosea and their three kids. Which is where we are at now. God tells Hosea the unimaginable. "Go find her Hosea," God says. "Go find her." What a heavy command. What a heart-wrenching request. But what I really want you to take a look at is what it says next. This part puts the whole thing in to perspective. *"Love her as the LORD loves the Israelites,"* (**verse 1**).

This might not mean much to you right now, but let me explain. God wants Hosea to pursue his unfaithful wife, just like God does to His people. Just like God did, and continues to do, for us. You see, where it says Israel it means Israel, but it's also speaking of God's love for the whole entire world. When we are saved, we become a part of Israel. We become adopted, and anytime you see God talk about Israel, it also means us (in context). God tells Hosea to love Gomer, this unfaithful wife, just like God loves us. And yes, men, He loves us even at our worst in life. He loves us when we really mess up. And He loved Israel even though they turned to other gods and loved the sacred raisin cakes. In other words, even when they turned to get their fulfillment from other things in this world, He still loved them and passionately pursued them.

Verse 2 he continues to write, *"So I bought her for fifteen shekels of silver and about a homer and a lethek of barley."* What a second. He bought her?? Hosea bought his wife back? You might be thinking, wait, how can you buy something that already belongs to you?! That's his wife and

he has to buy her back?? Go in there and bust everyone up.
Tear down their tents. Kidnap her when they are not
looking. Call Liam Neeson! Why should he have to buy
back his own wife? We don't really read in detail what
Hosea was thinking or what was going through his mind
right about now, but I have a feeling it must have been
hard. This man had to buy his wife back from the slave
trading industry.

Now, if you haven't figured it out yet, Hosea is a
picture of God and sadly, you and I are a picture of Gomer.
And in case you didn't know, this is exactly what God did
for us. He went on a messy pursuit to reconcile us back into
His love. Even though we left God, pursued other things,
and ignored him, we were still His creation. He was still
our creator. He made us! The bible tells us, *"The earth is
the Lord's, and everything in it, the world, and all who live
in it,"* (**Psalm 24:1; see 1 Corinthians 10:26**) and yet our
God paid an overwhelming price for us. He paid for what
he already possessed and he sent his son, Jesus Christ, to
die for us. Our Savior shed his blood to purchase back what
God already owned. He didn't have to, He chose to.

When I think about this, I tend to hang my head in
awe. No doubt Gomer hung her head in embarrassment and
shame. She abandoned him. She abandoned their three
kids. She left him, yet he insisted on buying her back. To
the world, it doesn't make sense. To me, it didn't make
sense for the longest time. How could one do this? How
does one master a painful predicament like this? But get
this men, it doesn't end there.

In **verse 3,** Hosea basically renews his vows towards her. *"Then I told her, 'You are to live with me many days; you must not be a prostitute or be intimate with any man, and I will behave the same way toward you.'"* Much like God, Hosea went above and beyond. Not only did God send Jesus to forgive us of our sin, He sent Jesus to completely redeem us from the Curse of the Law. He freed us from the bondage of sin and the bondage of the devil. He made us Righteous and blameless before the throne, by the blood of His one and only Son, Jesus Christ. He brought us in and out of the storm, gave us warm clothes, fed us, and adopted us, making sure we never have to be alone ever again. When we were considered "unlovable" by the world, God stepped in and said, "No, I still love them and I still want them!" If that's not true love then I don't know what is!

Real love, real men

Men, anyone can walk away from a situation like this. It takes someone of great strength to love unconditionally. Judah Smith said it like this, "These other men wanted to buy her to use her. Hosea wanted to buy her to heal her."[3] Wow. This right there is agape love; unconditional love. Hosea loved her even when the world would have told him to walk away. "You don't deserve this, Hosea. Just leave and find yourself someone who will truly love you." But he didn't. He swallowed his pride and took her back. He loved her with the God kind of love.

Even though we were filthy and broken and evil, God came after us. He came down into this sin-filled earth and did whatever it took to reconcile us. He pursued us, bought us, and renewed his vows telling us, *"I will make my dwelling among you and walk among you, and I will be your God, and you will be my people,"* (see **2 Corinthians 6:16**).

The big picture

I want you to see this picture. I want you to see this picture more than anything and to try and envision the strength and love it would take to go back for someone who hurt you and repeatedly abandoned you, yet you insist on finding them and holding them and loving them. Honestly, for me it would be hard. I would need God's strength. I couldn't do it by myself. We have all been hurt before, and we have all been to the point where we just didn't want to deal with them anymore. Like I said, we were Gomer. We were the ones that had been unfaithful. We were the ones who betrayed God over and over again. We were the ones who left God in pursuit of the world and its desires.

You may be running from God right now. You may be trying to find purpose in the things of this world; whether it be money, girls, a job, drugs, whatever it may be. Maybe you fell away hard and sometimes you think about going back, but you wonder if God would even take you back. You might even be walking with God right not, but you keep sinning in one area, thinking that God is disappointed in you. Wondering if you will ever be good enough. You may honestly just have no clue what God thinks about you. I am here to say HE LOVES YOU.

Jesus came and died for us even at our darkest time. The children of Israel continually fell away and chased after other gods, but God sent prophet after prophet to warn them to repent and to come back to him. Over and over again God asked His children to come back to Him. And you know, God made sure the story of Hosea and Gomer was placed in the Bible for us to read so that we can be reminded of His mercy and love for us. It was placed there to show you that no matter where you are at, it's not too late to turn back to God. In fact, He is pursuing you, meeting you where you are at. You might be in a dark place right now, but God will still meet you there. Just like Hosea came after Gomer, God's mission is to come after you, but not to judge you or condemn you (see **John 3:17**); He seeks you to heal you, to redeem you, to give you life. It doesn't make sense does it? But that's what grace is... It's scandalous.

All we were ever taught as children was that bad people get bad things and good people get good things, but Jesus came to give us all a second chance at life, no matter what we have done or where we are at in our lives. He loves you, whether you choose to believe it or not, He adores you. He doesn't see us as we see ourselves, which is why He wants us to start seeing things as He sees them.

It reminds me of a story I heard my co-worker tell. He was talking about this woman who had been in and out of jail numerous times. Someone he knew was "dating" her but he didn't like that idea because of her past. His friend stated, "But she has been reading the Bible!" My co-worker responded, "Everyone reads the Bible in jail. That's because God is the only person who would take them back. That's the only person who would forgive her! That's her only option." I sat there and thought about it for a bit. You know, everyone in the world could reject you, they could abandon you, and they could forget you, but there will always be that one person who will forgive you and take you back: Jesus. He is so merciful. Whether anyone believes you are really changed or not, don't worry. God knows. That's all that really matters, right? Hey, he thinks you are to die for... literally.

The prodigal son

This passage in Luke is among the stories Jesus tells us after being asked the question, "Why do you hang out with bad people?" Jesus tells the story of the lost coin, the lost sheep, and the last story that is a little different; it's a story about the lost son. You may have heard this story before, but I want to look at it a little deeper. This story is actually about two sons, in which one son decides he wants his inheritance early. His father gives it to him and he leaves to live in the city.

The son eventually wastes all his money away and finds himself working on a farm where he fed pigs. Talk about an all-time low. He was so hungry and so poor that even what the pigs were eating looked good. But then this son came to his senses and he had an idea. "How many of my father's hired men have food to spare, and here I am starving to death! I will set out and go back to my father." So he thought up a speech to tell his father.

Luke 15:20 tells us, *"So he got up and went to his father. But while he was still a long way off, his father saw him and was filled with compassion for him; he ran to his son, threw his arms around him and kissed him. The son said to him, 'Father,'* he starts in to his rehearsed speech, *'I have sinned against heaven and against you. I am no longer worthy to be called your son.' But the father said to his servants, 'Quick! Bring me the best robe and put it on him. Put a ring on his finger and sandals on his feet. Bring the fattened calf and kill it. Let's have a feast and celebrate.'"*

Now, I want you to see a couple things. First, this son hit rock bottom. He lost it all. He went and sought out the things of this world and found out that they hold no real value. So he developed a plan. He had a speech all planned out to deliver to his father. He was going to return to his father who would hopefully have some mercy for him and allow him to at least be his servant. The Bible tells us that as the son was still a long way off, the father saw him and RAN TO HIM; he met his son where he was. The father didn't wait for him to get there, he was so excited to see his son, no matter what mistakes he made, that he ran to him and embraced him with open arms.

You see, men, back in the day Jews considered this highly undignified in their culture. The father/leader never ran or never made the first move in such a situation as this. Yet this paints a beautiful picture of how God sees us. God the Father sought us and ran to us, without holding our mistakes against us. He breaks the boundaries of so called "religion" and shows us what a real relationship with God is all about. But the part that amazes me the most is that the son tries and gives the speech that he rehearsed, yet he doesn't even finish it. The father interrupts him and calls for his servants to grab the best robe and put it on his son. He calls them to put a ring on his finger and sandals on his feet and to bring the fattened calf and kill it. In other words he is saying, "let's get this party started!" But there is even more depth to this. I want you to look at the things the father was preparing for his son. Each one of these things actually has a deeper meaning to it.

"Bring forth the best robe and put it on him"
When the father ordered the best robe to be placed on him, the Father was pretty much telling the Prodigal son and anyone who saw this event that his place as son was being completely restored. This act was an intimate demonstration of the father basically saying, "Here is my complete approval, my complete love, and my complete mercy to you." This son who was once lost was being restored back to his position, without any condemnation for the careless mistakes and hurt he had caused before.

As I researched, I noticed the same thing happened in **Genesis 27:15**. Rebekah, Jacob's wife, took the best clothes of Esau, the oldest son, and put them on Jacob, the younger son. You see, back in the Hebrew culture most or all property, inheritance and blessing went to the oldest son, also called the firstborn. You definitely wanted to be the first born back then. After doing some more research, I also found it in **Zechariah 3:4-5** when God told Zechariah to take away Joshua's filthy garments and clothe him with fine garments or, in some translations, rich robes. I really like this one because it literally tells a story of a man going from rags to riches! Joshua found favor with God and any wrong doing or condemnation that may have been with him was completely removed from him. Dressed in rich garments/robes, Joshua stood clean and completely forgiven before God. Dressed in the best robe, the Prodigal Son stood clean and completely forgiven before his father.

"Put a ring on his hand" From research, in certain cultures, presenting a ring to someone was a sign of great affection, honor, and could also be a symbol of being placed in a position of authority. Two stories from the Bible come to mind when I think of rings. If you recall, Pharaoh removed his signet ring and put it on Joseph's hand when promoting him to the second most powerful man in all of Egypt (see **Genesis 41:42**). In the book of Esther, the King took off his royal ring and gave it to Mordecai, Esther's uncle (see **Esther 8:2**). The king would use this ring to sign laws and decrees.

When Pharaoh gave his ring to Joseph, it was his way of showing his affection and respect for him. Same thing between the king and Mordecai. They transferred to them all power and authority they needed for the positions they received. The ring the father gave to the son showed the same exact thing. It showed great affection and love the Father had toward him. He was basically saying, "Welcome back to the family."

And the last part here: **"Put sandals on his feet."** Anytime someone returns home with no shoes, you know they have had a couple of bad days. This son returned home without shoes on, a sure sign of having lost everything. You see, back in ancient biblical times, only servants and slaves went barefoot. Therefore, when the Father ordered shoes to be brought out and put on the son's feet, he said for the third and final time that his son was not to be treated as a servant. In fact, with all three of these signs of affection, the father was showing everyone that his son that was once lost is now back in the family. Everything he gave up was given back to him. Once again, this parable paints an amazingly beautiful picture of God's redeeming love for us.

The whole package deal

Forgiveness would be empty without restoration. Men, if you bear the name "son" through having received Jesus as Lord and Savior by the power of the Holy Spirit, you are forgiven. You are loved. You are redeemed, restored, healed, and highly favored. It's true. Everything changes.

#DearChristianMen, God has placed the robe on you. He has restored you. He has forgiven you. He has covered you with His love. You are made new. Men, a ring has been put on your finger declaring all the riches you now have in Christ. You have been given the name of Jesus, and with that everything has been given to you. You have been promoted to a higher office. You have been promoted to a new life; a life more abundant. And Men, the sandals that have been placed on your feet confirms sonship and every single benefit that comes with it.

When we are God's children we get the benefit of His **loving kindness, healing, prosperity, peace, mercy, joy** and **every other good thing He promises us in His word** (read **Psalm 103**).

Men, you are heirs of God and a joint heir with Christ Jesus who has been appointed heir of all things (see **Romans 8:17, Hebrews 1:2**). We have so many things to praise God for. Through Jesus, God did way more than most Christians even realize. With all that said, **Isaiah 61:10 (NKJV)** becomes our new banner. It becomes our daily praise. "*I will greatly rejoice in the Lord, my soul shall be joyful in my God; for He has clothed me with the garments of salvation, as a bridegroom decks himself with ornaments and as a bride adorns herself with her jewels.*"

The finale

After this the father says in **verse 24**, *"For this son of mine was dead and is alive again, he was lost and is found. So they began to celebrate."* How long did it take for them to start celebrating the son's return? Was it fifteen minutes? An hour? Two hours? No, Jesus tells us that they began to celebrate right after the father says these things. Men, when you repent and come back to God-when you truly come to Him with a heart to change-God doesn't hold it over your head. He doesn't make you wait it out until you learned your lesson. He doesn't put you in a corner and makes you think about your mistakes. He forgives you immediately after asking for forgiveness and you guys began to celebrate.

The Bible tells us that all of Heaven rejoices when a person comes to repentance (see **Luke 15:7**). You come before him, repent of your sin, ask for his forgiveness and it's done. So many times I have asked for forgiveness and He forgave me, then I start talking about it again, "Lord, why did I do that??" Do what?" God says to me. "The thing I just did!" God responds with, "What thing?" I just kind of sit there with this growing grin on my face. You know, the Bible tells us that God blots out our transgressions and chooses to remember our sins no more (see **Isaiah 43:25**). And honestly, He does.

I tried bringing back up the sin I was forgiven for, and it's like he has actually forgotten about it. I then realize I am talking about something that seriously is not even held against me anymore. I am no longer bound to that sin any more. And that is what this father did for his son. Immediately they begin to party like nothing happened. The only thing on the father's mind is the fact that his son was once lost but is now found.

#DearChristianMen, when you sin, the most powerful place you can be is wrapped in God's love. As humans, our natural response if we were the father in this parable would be placing our son in the corner and saying something like, "Don't you even think about having fun right now! Sit your butt in the corner and you can watch everyone else have fun. You think about your sin and what you have done." But not this father. He insisted that his son dance and enjoy. I am not saying we can get away with sin and abuse God's grace. I am not saying that we shouldn't discipline our kids. And I am not saying that sometimes there will be consequences for certain sin.

Listen to me, God's grace is not a credit card for sin. God's grace is empowerment to not want to sin; it's the empowerment to overcome. Jesus tells this story to get our minds off condemnation and to focus on the love that God has for us. He wants more than anything for us to come to Him, give Him our cares and anxieties, and to repent of our sin. He wants us to seek Him more and more every day; growing more mature as each day goes on. He desires to have a real relationship with you. He wants you to come to Him for the small things just as much as the big things. He wants to be a part of your everyday life. That's what Jesus is trying to get by here.

These religious leaders questioning Jesus were so consumed with the law that they thought that God's grace and mercy was too good to be true, but it's not. It's real and so is His everlasting love. There will be days of pain: seek Him. There will be days of complete joy: seek Him. There will be days of confusion: seek Him. And there will be days where everything seems to make sense: seek Him. Men, you need to get this in your mind. It is one of the greatest understandings you can ever gain: how much God loves you.

Without love, it means nothing

You know men, it's one thing to talk about love, it's another to imitate it. It's one thing to do something nice, it's another to truly mean it. The question is: was love at the center of your action? Have you ever had someone give you a gift that didn't really mean much to you because you could tell they didn't really want to give it to you? It's like that bully at school that is forced to apologize to you for picking on you and giving you a wedgie. The teacher pulls him over to you and tells him to apologize. He kind of mutters out a pathetic apology. Somewhere in the mumbling you somewhat comprehend the word "sorry," but you couldn't really tell. The dude didn't even make eye contact with you! The teacher accepts it and everyone goes on their way.

But you sit there and wonder what just happened. Obviously the kid didn't mean it, it was forced! That apology didn't mean that much to you because you know that the bully didn't truly say it with love. He wasn't truly sorry, rendering that apology worthless. It sounds harsh when you say it like that, but it's truth. We all have been there before. For me, I have been on both ends of that story. Though I wasn't a bully, I have made apologies before that I didn't really mean, which made them a lie, and therefore worthless.

The way Paul talked to the Church of Corinth in **1 Corinthians 13** tells me that they were just like this bully. They were doing good acts, but they needed to be reminded that if love was not the reason for doing the acts, then those acts didn't truly mean anything. Paul says it like this, *"If I speak in the tongues of men or of angels, but do not have love, I am only a resounding gong or a clanging cymbal. If I have the gift of prophecy and can fathom all mysteries and all knowledge, and if I have a faith that can move mountains, but do not have love, I am nothing. If I give all I possess to the poor and give over my body to hardship that I may boast, but do not have love, I gain nothing."*

Look how extreme Paul gets. We are talking about huge acts of faith here. We are talking about Christians who spoke in the language of angels or men, but did not love. They became nothing but a noisy sound. Ouch, right? You could be amazing at preaching and speaking, but it means absolutely nothing if you are not preaching in love.

I don't know about you, but I am thinking of some
people who go and picket funerals and talk about how
much God hates certain people. That right there is not love.
I can think of plenty of "Christians" who condemn and
judge non-Christians, and even other Christians, on a daily
basis. Love is not at the center of any of that, and therefore
it means nothing.

Paul even goes to the extreme to say that we could
fathom all mysteries and know all things, and even have
super faith to move mountains, but without love motivating
those things, we go nowhere. Men, we can give all we earn
away to the poor and needy, we can even go to the stake to
be burned as a martyr, but without love at the center of it
all, we gain nothing. Men, Paul makes these analogies seem
so extreme to show us how important this is. He is trying to
get a message through to a people who are just faking the
funk. Whatever you are doing right now in this life, if you
aren't doing it out of the love for Jesus and/or the love for
others, it means nothing.

Love is a big and powerful thing. It's the reason of
our existence. It's the reason we were saved. It's the reason
we live. Look at it this way. If God is love, then Paul
basically is stating this: Without God, all things are
worthless.

Love: the game changer

When it comes to loving people, I know sometimes it can be hard to love things that are unlovely, but I want you to try something. Actually, I want to give you a dare. Men, next time someone is mean or unlovely to you, I dare you to love them. Seriously. You heard me right. I dare you to love your enemy. I dare you to love the one who hates you, or is talking bad about you, or giving you attitude. I don't care if this person is screaming at the top of his or her lungs at you. Love them. Smile at them and let them know that it doesn't matter what they say or do, they can never do anything to make you hate them. This was a revelation God gave me one night. God dared me to do the same thing; to love on someone who was hating on me.

When we love those people, we may not see a change right away, but you just overcame evil; you just won. You see, when we choose to love, we choose to use a weapon that is designed and forged to win every single time. #DearChristianMen, love never fails (see **1 Corinthians 13:8**). So when we love no matter what, we come out victorious no matter what. Even if the discussion ends with them still yelling at you and giving you dirty looks, love won. You can never fail if you choose to love someone.

That's a secret weapon that many people don't understand they have. People think that not responding to someone yelling at you makes you look weak. They think that if you don't have a snappy come back, then you lost.

Maybe it does look weak from the outside, but deep down, it takes more strength and self-control to love someone who is hard to love, than it does to scream back at that same person. You see that, men? Love always wins. Love never fails. There is always victory when you choose to love. You may not feel like you won at first, but give it time. You will be surprised. Love changes people. Love touches even the hateful of humans.

It's only right to end this with my one of my favorite passages. It fits perfectly in this section and I honestly believe this sums up true Christianity perfectly. When we experience God's perfect love, it sets off a change and transformation inside of us that will show on the outside by our words and actions. I believe the more we mature in Christ, the more we will fit this role and these things will come natural to us. The more we start to look like this passage, the stronger the Church will be. Division would be broken, and people would see Jesus and want what we have: True Love. This passage comes from **Romans 12:9-21**.

Love must be sincere. Hate what is evil; cling to what is good. Be devoted to one another in love. Honor one another above yourselves. Never be lacking in zeal, but keep your spiritual fervor, serving the Lord. Be joyful in hope, patient in affliction, faithful in prayer. Share with the Lord's people who are in need. Practice hospitality.

Bless those who persecute you; bless and do not curse. Rejoice with those who rejoice; mourn with those who mourn. Live in harmony with one another. Do not be proud, but be willing to associate with people of low position. Do not be conceited. Do not repay anyone evil for evil. Be careful to do what is right in the eyes of everyone. If it is possible, as far as it depends on you, live at peace with everyone.

Do not take revenge, my dear friends, but leave room for God's wrath, for it is written: "It is mine to avenge; I will repay," says the Lord. On the contrary: "If your enemy is hungry, feed him; if he is thirsty, give him something to drink. In doing this, you will heap burning coals on his head." Do not be overcome by evil, but overcome evil with good.

In other words: *Love from the center of who you are; don't fake it. Run for dear life from evil; hold on for dear life to good. Be good friends who love deeply; practice playing second fiddle. Don't burn out; keep yourselves fueled and aflame.*

Be alert servants of the Master, cheerfully expectant. Don't quit in hard times; pray all the harder. Help needy Christians; be inventive in hospitality. Bless your enemies; no cursing under your breath. Laugh with your happy friends when they're happy; share tears when they're down.

Get along with each other; don't be stuck-up. Make friends with nobodies; don't be the great somebody. Don't hit back; discover beauty in everyone. If you've got it in you, get along with everybody. Don't insist on getting even; that's not for you to do. "I'll do the judging," says God. "I'll take care of it."

Our Scriptures tell us that if you see your enemy hungry, go buy that person lunch, or if he's thirsty, get him a drink. Your generosity will surprise him with goodness. <u>Don't let evil get the best of you; get the best of evil by doing good</u> (**Romans 12:9-21 MSG**).

7

THE PREVAILING CHURCH MAN

#DearChristianMen, I believe God wants to bring His Church into a time of prevailing, but we as men have to get ourselves in a prevailing mindset. He wants us to be constantly moving forward and growing. For example, Jesus came to earth to give us redemption and victory. But if you noticed, He spent a majority of His ministry preaching, teaching and preparing His people to have a mindset of redemption and victory. Many, if not all, did not have the mindset they needed to receive Jesus. God had to show them.

For those of you who don't know, prevailing means to approve more powerful against an opposing force; to be or prove superior in strength, power, or influence.[4] Men, God has created and called us to be more powerful than darkness; to be superior in **strength**, **power**, and **influence**. In other words, our life should reflect the Love of God so much, that it will influence anyone and everyone who comes in contact with us. The words we speak will lift others up instead of tearing them down. Our actions will encourage and convict others to live a life worthy of the calling. Our overflowing joy will give others hope. And the peace that we have through the storms of this life will get others asking, "Who is this guy and why is he always happy? I want what he has!"

Our influence will be greater than that of the devil's. And the more men we get prevailing, the more the Church will begin to prevail, and when the church starts prevailing, the more souls we will save. But it starts with us. It starts with renewing our minds and wanting it more than anything. Do you want to be better? Do you want to grow? Do you want to see the sick healed and the lame walk? Do you want to see the mute speak and blind eyes opened? Do you desire to see captives set free and love overcoming hate? Do you want to see your family prospering? Do you want your life to be a beacon of hope in this dark world? Do you want to see your marriage come alive and flourish? Then it starts here.

Be a light

If any of you are from the Midwest then you will know exactly what I am talking about. Our winters are not fun. It's cold, it's wet, and just windy. But I think the worse part about the winter here is the lack of sunlight. There are many days where the clouds are just too thick, and it's dark and dreary out. You just don't feel like doing anything. It's like the darkness drains you of any excitement and energy. But once that sun comes out, something happens. People start moving around and going places. You feel motivated to go out and be active. When Spring hits around here and the sun starts shining, it doesn't matter if it's still 40 degrees out, people are outside doing stuff.

Where am I getting at with this? There is something about the light that brings life. And as you and I go out into this dark world, we are called to shine our light (see **Matthew 5:14**). We are called to make a change in the world and bring energy and joy. We are called to prevail. Everywhere we go we should be bringing God's presence with us and influencing change. Men, THIS is prevailing.

The most high experience

Before my best friend truly gave his life to Christ, he was addicted to video games. That was his high. But one night, after he purchased a brand new video game, he finally decided to come to our church. After church during a one on one with our pastor, my pastor asked him something that would change his mindset forever. He asked, "Why are you doing these things? Do you get a high off of it? What is it? You know what a real high is? Seeing people who have been bound by the enemy for years become healed and whole; free from bondage. To see bones and ligaments restored and demons casted out of people. THAT is the ultimate high that surpasses all others."

After that night my friend was forever changed. He went home and broke his brand new video game disc and sold his console. He fell in love with God and never looked back. He wanted to see people give their life to the Lord more than to have a kill streak. Men, a prevailing man sees and understands what real fulfillment is. His mindset goes beyond the temporary and into the eternal. Those rankings and trophies will only last a little while compared to the eternal rewards you will receive for what you did in this life.

The gates of hell shall not prevail

Matthew 16:18 (ESV), "*And I tell you, you are Peter, and on this rock I will build my church, and the gates of hell shall not prevail against it.*" The Church is not a building, it's not a sign over the door, it's not a denomination, and it's not a certain race. The Church is anyone who has truly accepted Jesus as their Lord and Savior. So if you have accepted Jesus, then YOU are a member of the Body of Christ, which makes up the Church. According to this scripture, Jesus Himself tells us that the gates of hell will not prevail against us. In other words, we are the ones who need to prevail against the gates of hell; we need to step up and fight. The only way hell can overcome us is if we let it. Sadly, there are so many Christians out there who are letting the enemy trample over them. They just live their lives getting pushed around by the devil, just hoping they make it to heaven.

#DearChristianMen, God did not call us to limp into heaven. We were called to prevail; to overcome hell and all its schemes. Christians were not meant to build an ark and weather the storm. Instead, we were created to push back the forces of darkness and take it by force. Somewhere along the lines we started to think that humility means to lay down and take it, and "meek" means "weak." We started to develop this mindset where we curl up in a ball and just hold out. I can assure you, men, we were created to be loving towards people, but have a righteous anger towards the devil and his schemes. Jesus himself told His disciples, "*I have given you authority to trample on snakes and scorpions and to overcome all the power of the enemy; nothing will harm you* (**Luke 10:19**)."

The problem

Here are two problems with Christians now days:

1) They are not being taught the true anointed word of God. Many Christians are attending churches that only teach milk and no meat. Milk is not necessarily bad, but at some point, Christians need meat to grow; we cannot live off of milk alone. In fact, a lot of teachings are watered down by the doctrines of men. They teach off of experiences rather than the Word of God. In other words; they nullify the word of God by tradition that they have handed down (see **Mark 7:13**). This is truth. Men's doctrines and traditions have caused the Word of God to be of no effect; to seem powerless.

Have you ever drank a soda that has been watered down? Doesn't taste good does it? Honestly, a lot of times people tend to follow man instead of God. It all derives from watered-down teachings from men. **Hebrews 5:11-14** says, *"We have much to say about this, but it is hard to explain because you are slow to learn. In fact, though by this time you ought to be teachers, you need someone to teach you the elementary truths of God's word all over again. You need milk, not solid food! Anyone who lives on milk, being still an infant, is not acquainted with the teaching about righteousness. Solid food is for the mature, who by constant use have trained themselves to distinguish good from evil."*

The author of Hebrews is saying that so many of these followers of Christ should have been teachers already, but they were not grabbing hold of it. They needed to be taught elementary things all over again (milk). Anyone who is constantly living on milk is still an infant in Christ. And no offense, you can be grown but that doesn't make you a man. I have seen many grown men and women in church who have been going for years, but that doesn't mean they are spiritually mature. You can have a job, car, and a house but it does not mean you have become a man of God. Solid food is for the mature, those who have trained themselves up to understand good from evil.

I do understand though, in many cases it's not their fault. Their leaders are constantly feeding their congregation milk instead of meat. But at the same time, we all need to be reading our Bibles so we can determine right from wrong. We need to be diving into God's word on our own time as well. Every day and every night we should be meditating on His word and growing deeper and deeper in

Christ. It's sad how many Christians don't actually read their Bibles. It's one of those things that may not be easy at first, but once you grab a hold of it, it is completely worth it. God's Word changes things.

2) In other situations, people are being taught the truth, yet they reject it or do not hold on to it. They are perfectly fine where they are at and they don't want to grow, they don't want to be challenged, and they surely do not want to exercise faith. So many Christians just want to go to a church that will allow them to stay in their comfort zone and "just get by." It's just being lazy. *"My people are destroyed from lack of knowledge and because you have rejected knowledge,"* (see **Hosea 4:6**).

These two reasons are why the church is not prevailing as it should. They step back at the first sign of trial. They step back when they realize they have to give up things. They do not see the whole picture of victory. They fear change. But if you could only see what the real Church should look like, you wouldn't fear at all. The Body of Christ tends to grab on to the wrong parts of teachings; we grab on to the false humility side of things rather than the true victory that Christ gives us. Say for instance, Paul's thorn in the flesh. If you are not familiar with this story then you can read it in **2 Corinthians 12**. It says that Paul had a thorn in the flesh. It wasn't an actual thorn, but the Bible tells us it was a "messenger of Satan."

The Greek word for "messenger" tells us that it was an angel. In other words, Paul was being attacked by a demonic force. This demonic force would go ahead of Paul on his journey and stir up strife in the crowds towards him. It was there to try and keep him from being puffed up due to the fact that he had been receiving great revelation knowledge. And if you have read the story of Paul, you know that he was beaten, mocked, stoned, left for dead, and the list goes on. But what did he do? He got back up and asked God for more boldness to preach His word. There was even one point that Paul was thought to be dead and they drug him out of the city, but he got back up and headed back into the city.

Gentlemen, THAT is prevailing against the enemy. No matter what the devil did against Paul to try and stop him, he got back up and continued the battle, spreading the Good News about Jesus. He did not fear death, hell, or the grave. It didn't matter what people thought of him, he continued to fight back and prevail. That's what being a man of God is about; never giving up. Too many times we are so afraid to die for Christ that we are not truly ready to live for Him. #DearChristianMen, we have to understand that we are called to be victorious over the enemy and to prevail in the area God calls us. But many only grab part of this story.

They grab on to the part where Paul asks God to remove this thorn in the flesh three times and God responds, "*My grace is sufficient for you, for my power is made perfect in weakness* (**Verse 9**)." They think that God said "No" to Paul. They see it as God telling Paul it's better that he is being attacked and that he just needs to hold out.

But the word "no" is not in any translation of the Bible. God wasn't denying Paul of healing or victory. In fact, God was telling Paul, "My grace is all you need to overcome this. My power comes alive when we are weak. Jesus, grace in the flesh, is all you need and He is yours!"

God was giving Paul the ultimate blessing and reminder that when we come across trials, WE are the ones who need to stand up and grab a hold of God's strength and prevail against the enemy and his schemes! God has given us everything we need to live a prevailing life. Paul understood that and knew he could boast in his weakness because God's power was made perfect in those moments. He knew that he could accomplish anything, and if it didn't seem like he could, God's power would step in and help him complete the task. He could glorify God in his strength and glorify God in his weaknesses. It was a win-win for Paul. I know there are many Christians who don't believe what I just said, but it's right there in the Bible. We have to rightly divide the word of God, not twist it and try to make it fit our own lifestyle and way of thinking. Paul even writes in **2 Timothy 3** about his persecutions and sufferings he went through, but ends **verse 11** with, "*Yet the Lord rescued me from all of them.*"

Men, I am not trying to say you won't have some bad days. We will be persecuted. We will suffer for Christ. We will be hated and have trials and tribulation and there may even come a time in our lives we will need to ask ourselves, "Would I truly die for Christ?" But when we trust in God and draw our strength from Him, He will give us the victory every single time. We will prove to be stronger, more powerful, and more influential than anything the enemy throws at us.

#YouCantStopMe

In **Philippians 1**, Paul is writing this letter while in chains. He is imprisoned because he was preaching the gospel. "But CJ, that doesn't sound like prevailing to me." Well, let's read what Paul has to say about it in **Philippians 1:12**, *"Now I want you to know, brothers, that what has happened to me has really served to advance the gospel. As a result, it has become clear throughout the whole palace guard and to everyone else that I am in chains for Christ. Because of my chains, most of the brothers in the Lord have been encouraged to speak the word of God more courageously and fearlessly."* THIS my brothers is prevailing.

How many of us, if we were put in prison for preaching the gospel, would have this kind of attitude? I kind of have a feeling a lot of us would be like, "Why me, God? Why does this always happen to me???" You know it's probably true. But Paul, no matter what came at him, prevailed. Even while in chains he continued to influence those around him. The whole prison knew who Paul was living for. Word even got out and fellow Christians began to preach with more courage and boldness.

#DearChristianMen, a prevailing man is not moved by his circumstances. He continues to preach God's word, courageously and fearlessly, while influencing anyone and everyone around him. Paul's life caught the attention of even his enemies. His Christian life rocked every city he went to. This is a prevailing man. We should be game changers; one who overcomes any obstacle the enemy sets before him.

Men, we were created and designed to prevail. To live a life worthy of the Lord so that we may please him in every way: <u>bearing fruit</u> in **every** good work, <u>growing</u> in the knowledge of God, <u>being strengthened</u> with **all power** according to his glorious might so that you may have **great endurance** and **patience**, and <u>giving joyful thanks</u> to the Father, who has qualified you to share in the inheritance of his holy people in the kingdom of light (see **Colossians 1:10-12**). This is what a prevailing man looks like.

No slave mindset here!

Joseph was a great man of God. He was the kind of guy that no matter what you did to him, he would find a way to be victorious. Of course, it was God who was with him and it was God who showed him favor. But you couldn't keep this man down. This part actually isn't about Joseph at all, even though he was a great example of what a man of God is about. The story I want to get to actually takes place long after Joseph and his rise to fame in Egypt.

You see, because Joseph had God on his side, all of Egypt was blessed. Through 7 years of famine, God told Joseph how to get through it with abundance. Pharaoh made Joseph his right hand man, making him the second most powerful man in all the world. But once Joseph died and his fruitful and multiplying generation of children as well, the new king did not know who this Joseph guy was and who he lived for (God). He saw the Israelites (God's children) as a threat because of their great numbers, so he made them into slaves, putting slave masters over them and oppressing them with forced labor. This went on for 400 years.

Think about that. They were enslaved for about twenty generations! These kids were born in slavery. That's all their parents knew; the life of a slave. Their grandparents were slaves and their great grandparents were slaves. That's what they thought life was all about. You think they grew up saying, "I think I am going to be a doctor or a lawyer when I grow up,"? That was not an option for them. For 400 years, they had a slave mentality. There was no hope to anyone rising up and abolishing this way of life. They were too scared, too weak, and too insecure. They were defeated and that's the way they had always seen it… until Moses came along. God could use Moses. Why? Because he was not born into slavery.

You see, Moses was an Israelite, but if you remember, his mother put him in a basket and placed him in the Nile. When an Egyptian found him, they took him in and trained him up in royalty (his own mother actually nursed him until he grew a little. Then Pharaoh's daughter took him into the palace to raise him as her own. See **Exodus 2**). Are you starting to see where I am going? God could use Moses because he didn't have a slave mindset. He had some insecurities, but who doesn't? He didn't know bondage. He didn't know oppression. He was raised as royalty. He didn't have this "woe is me. I am just a slave, not worthy of anything or anyone" attitude.

Here's the deal: there are quite a few men out there who can't be used by God because they won't let God use them and change them. They do not see themselves as a prevailing man. We get so set in our ways that we would rather live in the sureness of our mediocre lifestyle than the possibility of greatness. Fear will always make you want to go back into bondage. Fear will always make you want to settle for less. Fear will always pull you away from the good things of God.

When Moses led the Israelites into the Promise Land, he sent out scouts to check out the land. When they saw their enemies, all were scared except Caleb and Joshua. **Numbers 14:1-4** says, *"That night all the people of the community raised their voices and wept aloud. All the Israelites grumbled against Moses and Aaron, and the whole assembly said to them, "If only we had died in Egypt! Or in this desert! Why is the LORD bringing us to this land only to let us fall by the sword? Our wives and children will be taken as plunder. Wouldn't it be better for us to go back*

to Egypt?" And they said to each other, "<u>We should choose</u>
<u>a leader and go back to Egypt.</u>"

What!? Are you serious? Go back to Egypt? You
mean go back to the place where you were SLAVES for
400 years? Yup, that's the place. The people of God were
in so much fear that they were willing to go back into the
bondage of the Egyptians again. They wanted the easy way
out, back into slavery rather than to have faith and step out
for their freedom.

Men, we cannot prevail with this mindset. Laziness,
fear, contentment in comfort; these things will destroy you
and send you back into bondage. Will you get to heaven?
Sure. But will you get others saved and find victory in your
life? Probably not. I'm not trying to judge or tear anyone
down. I'm not being blasphemous or mean. I am simply
stating the truth. You have a great calling on your life, men,
but only you can make the choice to throw off everything
that hinders and the sin that so easily entangles and run
with perseverance the race marked out for you (see
Hebrews 12:1).

We can either be a Moses, Joshua, or Caleb, and
fight for the promises of God, or we can be the grumbling
Israelites and give up at the first sign of pressure. I am
going to be honest, it's easier to just give up. But the
reward for pressing on is far greater than anything a
mediocre life has to offer.

The war within

Our war is not against flesh and blood, men. Our war is against the rulers, against the authorities, against the powers of this dark world, and against spiritual forces of evil in the heavenly realms (see **Ephesians 6:12**). We have to be aware that the things we battle in life are more spiritual than physical. Anger, strife, jealousy, and temptation; they are all spiritual battles that rage inside of us. But the good news is that we have been given power to overcome these forces. You don't have to surrender to them. You do not have to give up. We have been blessed too much to just want to be comfortable in this life.

A lot of churches today do not want to fight. We are called to battle. Our motto is not "Well, there is nothing we can do about it." No, we can do something about it. The question I ask you is: Are *you* going to do something about it? Generations before us had to fight for our freedom. They grew up with the mentality to fight and battle on, but these past couple generations have not had to do that. We didn't have to fight for the things we have, so we don't want to fight. We are very comfortable and the spirit of comfort and entertainment has perpetrated the church world and we don't want to fight. But remember what prevail means? It means that we prove more powerful than opposing forces.

Men, if we are going to serve God, there is going to have to be some resistance against the works of hell in your life. We need to be hooked up with a group of people who know how to prevail. Maybe you're in the same boat I am in. You see, I am tired of the testimonies that sound like this: "A sister had cancer and she lost the battle but God gave her family grace," or, "Well, they lost their house to a fire but hey, they are learning through it," or even, "Our business went under but we are still praising God." I understand there are times when things do not go as we planned and we have to move on and grow through it, but hear me out. I love to hear those testimonies where the children of God won! Where Satan tried to pull a fast one but we stood in faith and God blessed us through the storm.

I believe God wants the Church to be prevailing over the enemy. When our schools are overrun by drugs, when our friends are falling away, when the TV has nothing but sex, drugs and power on it, and we don't like where our nation is going, we just don't say, "Well, what can we do?" No, instead we stand our ground and grab a hold of what God has given us and we fight against it! Instead of giving up, we stand up! We are called to prevail!

Men, let me give you some encouragement. I have been on fire for the Lord for about 6 years now and I am still learning new things every single day. Some days are rough. Some days I feel so immature and lazy. But men, here's the thing, when we got saved, did we become men of God right away? Were we mature in the Lord right then and there? Of course not! We may not have seen signs of maturity until weeks, months, maybe even years after that. It took time to train ourselves on how God wants us to act. Do not get discouraged if you want to make a change but you do not see a complete transformation in days. Make the commitment and press forward, never giving up.

Pay day without the work days

#DearChristianMen, we talk about becoming a man and we pray about becoming a man, but we expect manhood to just fall on us. It takes time and diligence. We need to work at it just like we would train for a marathon. None of us sit around and eat junk food and then go out and successfully run a marathon. Unless you are super human, it doesn't work like that. When Christ died for us, we were not men right away. Christ freed us from the bondages of our sin and our past. We were no longer defined by who we were or how we acted. By His death, He enabled us to become men. He gave us the power and ability to change. He gave us a second chance at life. It's not going to come overnight. So stop comparing yourselves to other men. Men, stop comparing your "success" to another man's success. If we focus on Jesus Christ and the man he was, then He will show us how to act, how to talk, and how to love. The only way to prevail is to be like Christ, which takes time.

Wages without labor

In this day and age, men want results without putting in work. We want the power of God without having to use faith. We want to be teachers before being the student. But in order to reach maturity, we have to be willing to learn, which takes humility. A true disciple takes all the things he has learned from the Word of God and he applies it to his life. He doesn't just read about Christ, but he diligently and earnestly seeks to live out his life, just like Christ lived out His life. He doesn't just learn about love, but he seeks to become love. It's one thing to know truth, we must become walking and talking truth. We must study the Master (Jesus) in order to be transformed into the image of the Master.

We do not want to be those men who study Jesus and read about Him, but never seek to be like Him. We do not want to be men who study, read, and talk about love, yet never truly love. And men, we do not want to be those who read and know about the truth, yet do not act it out in our lives. Those men talk about sacrifice but do not develop a sacrificial lifestyle. They learn about serving but never really serve. To become a disciple of Jesus means to humble yourself and be ready to be corrected and learn. Is it always fun? No, but it's always worth it.

That is the biggest problem with many men today, they are not willing to learn and act on what they were taught. They think they are fine where they are, but we both know that they are slaves to their lifestyles. They have big visions but small work ethics. We want more revelation knowledge, but we haven't even done anything with what God already gave us!

We think we deserve the things of God when we do not do the things He require of us. Like the title of this section, too many men want their wages without having to do the labor.

#DearChristianMen, we are called not only to be present, but to lead, equip, guide and sharpen. We are called to prevail and influence the world around us. When other Christian men see those men who prevail in faith, hope, love, and truth, then they will be influenced and encouraged to stand up as well and become who they were called to be. We need to be bold though.

When I was working at the hospital as an ER Tech, I knew the truth but I was a little scared to stand up for what I believed. If I got rejected, I had to work with these people for a 12 hour shift! I didn't want them to judge me every time I passed by them. I remember one night, some nurses were talking about TV shows, video games, and movies. They asked me what I liked to watch and what video games I played. I told them that I didn't watch much TV and I don't really play video games anymore. I explained to them that I realized I had better things to do; that I could use that time to read my Bible or pray. I went on to tell them that I used to be a huge video gamer, but I sold all my stuff because it was taking up too much of my time. Video games was my unhealthy escape. That's all I would think about, but God delivered me from that.

They all looked at me weird, but I continued on working. It was slow that night and I was working with a doctor I had never worked with before. Later that night he pulled me to the side and told me he heard what I said about TV and video games. He was a Christian as well and explained to me how what I said was a blessing to him. It encouraged him to know that there were men out there who really did love God and wanted to seek Him any chance they had.

To you, that may not seem like much of an accomplishment, but for me it was. I was nervous to share that about my life because of what others may say and the arguments they may bring against me, but I said it anyway and without even knowing, someone was listening and it was encouraging to them. That right there meant more to me than all the TV shows and video games in the world. In that very moment, I was prevailing and influencing those around me, whether I knew it or not.

You have to want it more

Men's Devotional Bible by Zondervan told a story about a cowboy in Montana who was extremely good at bull riding.[5] This guy was legit. The way he was able to stay on that angry bull just amazed you. After a show, a reporter asked him, "What's your secret to being a great bull rider?" The cowboy pushed back is hat and grinned, saying, "You just gotta want to hang on more than the bull wants to throw you off." If you think about it, this makes sense in just about every area. Many times we like to make excuses, "I just don't have time for church," or, "I am just so busy with work and school." I understand we all have some busy schedules sometimes, but in all truth: if you really want it, you will make time. In other words, what this cowboy said was true: in order to prevail in this life, we have to want it more than anything. We have to want it more than the opposing force.

For me, I am a busy man, but when I really dissect my schedule, I have plenty of time to read my Bible and pray. There is no excuse for me to make about not having enough time to go deeper with Christ. If I really want to, I would do it. Some men are too tired to go to church, but will wake up at 3 a.m. to go hunting all day.

Trust me men, none of us can stand before God one day and give a good enough excuse to make God say, "Oh man, I guess you're right. You really didn't have enough time to get to know me. My bad. Well done, good and faithful servant." It's not going to happen like that. Like I said, the devil wants you to make these excuses. He wants you to fall and fail. He wants you to become lazy and comfortable. He desires more than anything to make you sin and feel guilty. Which is why you have to want to know God more than the devil wants to destroy you. That's right, men. You have to want it more.

To rephrase what that wise cowboy said, "You have to hang on to God more than the enemy wants to pull you away from Him." When you reach that mindset, then and only then, will you begin to prevail in Jesus' name.

You will do greater things

A famous man once said, *"Most assuredly, I say to you, he who believes in Me, the works that I do he will do also; and greater works than these he will do, because I go to My Father. And whatever you ask in My name, that I will do, that the Father may be glorified in the Son. If you ask anything in My name, I will do it."* In case you missed it, it was Jesus who said that in **John 14:12 (NKJV)**. What "works" is he talking about? He is actually talking about his preaching, his teaching, his loving, and his signs and miracles. For real. Of course, it's not by our own works, it's Him in and through us.

A prevailing man is one that prevails by the power of God, not by his own power. True victory comes through Christ and only through Jesus Christ. It's not spooky or weird, it's what we were told to do. There is nothing wrong with being gifted in speaking, but many churches throw out the signs and miracles and try to save people by mere talk alone through their own strength. Paul wrote to the Corinthians in **1 Corinthian 2:4**, saying, *"My message and my preaching were not with wise and persuasive words, but with a demonstration of the Spirit's power, so that your faith might not rest on human wisdom, but on God's power."*

Paul knew the power of God, and he knew that mere talk was not going to bring people to the knowledge of God. He presented the gospel with less of him and more of God; with power and mighty works, so that no one would put their faith into men, but God alone.

The thing you have to realize about Jesus' ministry is that He never used any typical method of publicity. He didn't hand out flyers, he didn't draw people in by games and a movie, and He didn't go out and hunt people down and try to bring them in. Not that these are bad, but He didn't need to do that. They just flocked to Him. There was no natural explanation for Jesus' successful ministry. How did it happen? Why was it so successful? It was God's power that promoted Jesus. And He used unnatural means to do it. Actually, He goes beyond unnatural and straight into the supernatural. It was not a matter of talk that brought the crowds, but the awesome manifestation of God's power (see **1 Corinthians 4:20**).

If you read in **Mark 1:21-28**, Jesus had just cast a demon out of a man at the synagogue in Capernaum a day before this event. This miracle, along with many others, caused the whole entire city to gather at Peter's house, and Jesus healed every single one of them (see **Luke 4:40).** Things like this happened all the time throughout His ministry. It was a way of life.

Jesus' display of the mighty power of God was the spark that ignited the curiosity in the hearts of those who saw and heard. Here's the kicker, and one of the main reasons I wrote this book: Jesus had this power because of His **intimate relationship** with God. He spoke with God daily and prayed daily. He only did what He saw His Father do and only said what He heard the Father say.

This is exactly what the life of a man of God should look like. We get so close and lost in God, that our lifestyle is a constant display of God's power. The words we speak, the actions we take, and everything we put our hand to is influenced directly from the Holy Spirit. People will see that and proclaim, "God has to be real." This is the calling of every single Christian man. If you're reading this, then this is for you. It's not just for preachers. It's not just for prophets. It's not just for leaders in the church. You are called to have an intimate relationship with the one, true God, just like Jesus did. You are called to prevail and have a prevailing ministry, just as Jesus did.

The FULL armor of God

"Put on the full armor of God, so that you can take your stand against the devil's schemes." (**Ephesians 5:11**)

Picture this: you are preparing yourself for battle. You are facing some of the most fierce warriors who are very good at what they do. You put on your chain mesh, slide your armor on over it. You strap your belt around your waist and tie everything together so it's held in place. You put on your helmet and grab your shield and sword. You are ready. You step on to the battle field and take a deep breath. This may be the last fight you ever fight. This is huge. You start to see the enemy come over the hill and your heart starts beating even faster. You began to sweat. It gets a little harder to breathe. But all of the sudden, you notice something weird about the enemy. As they get closer, you realize that they are not fully clothed. In fact, all they are wearing is a helmet. No sword, no shield, not even pants. Just a helmet. Yup, you read that right. They are completely naked except for a helmet.

I don't know about you but I think I would feel pretty good about fighting these enemies. A little disturbed, but pretty confident. Why? Come on, they are exposed! They are naked! They are not properly equipped for battle! There would be no way they could win. It would be a complete extermination. Here's the sad part. There are many Christians who are just like these warriors. They are running around with the Helmet of Salvation on, but that's it! As disturbing as that is, it's true. They are naked and completely vulnerable to the enemy. Saved? Sure. Victorious? Hardly.

They are so for salvation and they know they are saved, but they have no idea about the rest of the Armor of God. They are not sure about their righteousness in Christ, so they leave the breastplate home. They are not firmly rooted in the Truth of the Word, so they forget their belt. They are not fitted and ready to share the Gospel of Peace, so they throw their shoes back in the closet. They don't read their Bibles, so their Sword is left on the table. And they do not have any faith to withstand the blows of the enemy, so they keep the shield under their bed. These warriors are not fit for battle, which means they cannot stand against the devil's schemes.

Men, I don't want to make this more difficult than what it really is. Salvation is beautiful, but there is more to overcoming the devil than just being saved. Each piece of the Armor of God is vital to standing against the devil and his schemes. Each piece serves a very important and specific purpose.

Every morning we should prepare for battle against the enemy. The thing we have to remember is that the battle is between our ears. The greatest weapon Satan uses, and has ever used, is deception and lies. It's all a mind game with him. Men, we can never ever let our guard down. There's been times when I would go to church 3 to 4 times a week and I would feel great. I felt well fed and spiritually strong. I felt like I could take on the world. But then a thought would pop in my mind. "CJ, you have been to church so many times this week. You feel great. You feel empowered. Take some time to relax now and watch a movie. Go on the internet for a while. You're so filled right now you could even go a day without reading your Bible."

It sounds so dumb, but I would still let my guard down and succumb to the temptation of the enemy. I don't know if I am the only one who does this, but it happens more than I want it to. It's almost like me eating a huge meal today and then thinking, "Well, I just ate a really good, large meal. That should last me all month." It doesn't make sense. This mindset is a deception from the devil. Of course he wants you to let your guard down. Of course he wants you to relax. He wants you to get lazy. The devil does not want you to grow up in Christ. He doesn't want you to receive more revelation knowledge. And if he can keep you distracted from ever going deeper with God, then he has you right where he wants you. You're basically stuck in a never ending loop. It's like one step forward and two steps back.

This is why the Bible repeatedly tells us to stand firm, be alert, and to hold fast (see **1 Corinthians 6:13; 1 Peter 5:9; Colossians 1:23; 1 Thessalonians 2:15; Philippians 4:1**). It's ok to work, and it's ok to watch certain movies, and it's even ok to relax and take naps. I am not saying to keep looking over your shoulders in fear of the enemy. I am saying to wake up prepared every morning with a mind alert and ready to take on anything the devil throws at you that day. I am encouraging you to renew your mind daily; to go deeper with God. I am trying to teach you how to truly prevail every single day.

It reminds me of Gideon and his 300 men in the Old Testament. They were on hot pursuit of two kings for a long time. They battled and defeated every army that came against them. These guys were awesome! Of course, it was all glory to God. He gave them strength and power. But the Bible tells us that they were exhausted from pursuing these kings, yet they kept up with the pursuit (see **Judges 8:4**). They were tired, but they never stopped moving forward. They were on a mission for God and they knew they couldn't give up. Men, every morning when you wake up, you are on a mission for God. There will be things that exhaust you during the day, but you must push through. Put on the full armor of God. Why? So you can stand against everything the devil throws at you. Put on the full armor of God so that you can stand tall and prevail for the glory of God.

8

THE FALL OF MAN

#DearChristianMen, this world is not perfect. The awesome thing about the Bible is that it doesn't sugar coat things. There's murder, lust, war, sex, and power hungry men who would do anything to feed their pride. This book is a history lesson on the fall and redemption of mankind on the earth. It's not a fairytale and God warns us that it's not. It shows us flat out what man can and will do when they do not have God in their life. It shows us how selfish we are without God. And it shows us what the enemy is capable of when we give him a foothold in our lives.

In this fallen world we will experience difficulties. There will be storms in this life that try and wash you out to sea. And just because you are being attacked by the enemy doesn't always mean you have done something wrong. This is what Jesus tells us about in **John 16:33**. The writers of the New Testament, and even the Old Testament, warn us over and over again about this cursed world and what it's about. But why CJ? Even though we as Christians have been redeemed, this world has not. And there are certain things and areas, we as Men of God, need to avoid in order to continue on the path of righteousness.

Now, before we go on to the things that are harmful for men and women of God, I want to give a history lesson of the fall of man. I want to take you back to the days of Adam and Eve and the very first sin. I pray that you come to an even deeper understanding of God's true intentions for His creation and into a deeper understanding of how the enemy works in our lives to try and convince us that God is holding out on us. Let's begin.

In the beginning

God's plan for Adam and Eve in the beginning was beautiful. They were created to enjoy each other and their fellowship with God without any influence of evil. God did not want Adam and Eve to experience evil or even know about it. His original plan had no curse involved; no pain, no hurt, no suffering, no anger, no strife, no bitterness, and no sickness. However, we had Satan who rebelled against God and was basically trying to get Eve to join his little gang of rebels. Satan used the oldest lie in his playbook of deceit. What was that lie? That God is the ultimate killjoy who is trying to keep something good from you. Think about it. We all have thought this towards God sometime or another. The enemy has done a great job at convincing the world that God is a harsh God who is a complete fun sucker.

For me, when I got on fire for God, I broke up with my girlfriend and decided that I wanted to grow more in the Lord before I would get into another relationship. I told myself and God that the next woman I would pursue would be my future wife. There were times when I would meet a nice girl and think to myself, "Is this the one? Could she be it? She is awesome! I like talking to her. Wow, she has some white teeth." But every time that would happen, I felt God tell me "no," and I am going to be honest, I was a little upset. I thought she would make a great wife but God saw the whole picture. He saw what would happen if that relationship took off. He saw who she really was and He saw where I was truly at. Could it have worked out? Maybe. But God had different plans, and in my own little world I thought I knew best.

I thought God was holding out on me and maybe even being a buzz kill, but he wasn't. He had my best interests in mind and His plan for my life was far better than anything I could dream up. For those of you who are parents you may understand this a little bit.

My mom used to always tell me, "Put your seatbelt on," and I always thought she was a party pooper. Why didn't she understand that putting your seatbelt on was not cool and it always irritated my neck? But she was doing it because she had my best interests in mind. She knew that it was dangerous for me to not have it on and she knew what the result could be if I chose not to wear my seatbelt: injury or even worse, death. But me being young and ignorant, did not fully understand. One day we were pulling out of the grocery store onto a busy road and I decided to slip my seatbelt off when she wasn't looking. Well, my door must not have shut correctly because the door flew open and I rolled out of the car as we were turning the corner. I hit the concrete and rolled a couple times right into the busy street of oncoming traffic. My mom slammed on the breaks and got out. Before she even got to the other side of the car I was back inside in my seat, shaking in fear. I praise God I didn't hit my head or worse, get run over. I walked away with just a couple of scratches and an understanding of why I should put my seatbelt on.

You see, my mom was only trying to protect me just like God was trying to protect me from all the wrong relationships. He knew He had someone special for me. He knew the dangers of the wrong relationships, and He guided me out of those before they even started. Why? Because He loves me and you. I am so thankful I listened to Him because Leana, my soon-to-be-wife, is more than I could ever hope for. And He wants the same for you.

#DearChristianMen, God knows best. We need to stop thinking that we know more than Him or that we see the bigger picture more than God sees it. Men, stop playing god of your own little world. We make terrible gods, and the reason mankind fell in the first place was because we were tempted with the likeness of God, even though God had already created us in His image!

You know, I don't think Adam and Eve would have eaten that forbidden fruit if they hadn't been made dissatisfied with what they had. Through Satan's lie they were led to believe that they didn't have it all (see **Genesis 3:5**). The truth is, they did have it all. They were more like God before they ate of the fruit than after they ate the fruit. Satan tempts us in the same way he came against Adam and Eve (see **2 Corinthians 11:3**).

This is why it is so important to have a full revelation of our completeness in Christ. We need to understand what Christ died to give us, or should I say, returned to us. When we get this understanding it will keep us from chasing after all the things the devil has to offer. If anyone tells you that Christ isn't enough; that you need something more, then that's the enemy trying to turn you away from your completeness in Christ.

Satan's dirty little lie

Sometimes even a single question can get you to doubt God. Satan asked Eve, "Did God really say, 'You must not eat from any tree in the garden'?" (see **Genesis 3:1**) Eve told Satan they were not to eat of the forbidden fruit or they would die. Satan's reply to Eve suggested that God was a liar and that He just wanted to keep something good from them, saying, "*You will surely not die, For God knows that when you eat of it your eyes will be opened, and you will be like God,*" (see **Genesis 3:4, 5**)

Look what happens next, it tells us that the woman (Eve) *saw that the fruit of the tree was good for food and pleasing to the eye, and also desirable for gaining wisdom, she took some and ate it.* Does that sound familiar to you? John talks about this in **1 John 2:16** when he says, *"For all that is in the world—the lust of the flesh [craving for sensual gratification] and the lust of the eyes [greedy longings of the mind] and the pride of life [assurance in one's own resources or in the stability of earthly things]— these do not come from the Father but are from the world [itself]".*

Eve craved that sensual gratification of the flesh, was filled with greed, and desired the ability to have wisdom like God. Satan tempted her with it all and she went for it. She had no idea what she was giving up. If you read in the beginning, scriptures tell us that Adam and Eve walked with God through the garden (see **Genesis 3:8**). They had actual fellowship with God and talked with Him. Can you imagine? They walked and talked with God. A lot of us would give up the world in order to hear an audible voice from God every single day. Adam and Eve had that! But she ate of the fruit anyway and gave some to Adam.

Instead of giving up the world to get God, they gave up God to get the world. They gained knowledge of the difference between good and evil through direct experience, rather than being taught by God. We all know what happened next. Through that knowledge of evil, fear and shame entered the world, directly affecting Adam and Eve (see **Genesis 3:10**). Everything changed and the curse became rampant.

God knew exactly what He was doing when He told them to not eat of the Tree of Knowledge. This knowledge of good and evil was not a good thing. It ruined their innocent fellowship with God and each other. Men, God knows what He is doing. His Word, His commands, and His teachings were created to instruct us on how to live a holy and proper life. Whether you fully understand God's plan for your life, just know that He has the best and most fulfilled plan and purpose for you. *"No one whose hope is in you will ever be put to shame* (**Psalms 25:3**).*"* Anyone who trusts and believes in Jesus Christ will never ever be put to shame or be disappointed (see **Romans 10:11**).

Some of you may be thinking, "Why even create that tree in the first place?" And to others, you may be thinking that God set Adam and Eve up to fail from the start. I asked the same questions. I looked at the whole situation, and I even looked at this world and thought, "Why doesn't God just wipe out all evil?" Well someday He will completely wipe out all evil, but the thing is, God is love and when it comes to love there always has to be a choice.

You know, many Christians believe that God sets people up to fail. I have talked to countless people and their lack of knowing God's character has caused them to see God in a negative way. But what many people do not understand about why there is so much corruption in this world is because we have a free will: some choose God, others choose the world. God had to give Adam and Eve a choice. Without free will to choose, Adam and Eve would have just been puppets. That's not love. True love always requires choice. God wanted Adam and Eve to choose to love and trust Him. The only way to give this choice would have been to create something that was not allowed, giving them an option to choose from.

Since God planted lots of different trees in the garden to choose from, the test was not that difficult. Adam and Eve had plenty to eat and they had plenty of trees to choose from. Yet they chose that one tree that was forbidden. Just like us to want what we can't have, huh?

#DearChristianMen, God gives us a choice every day to live for Him or not. He will never force you. God loves you too much to make you follow His instructions. But His instructions are laid out for your benefit. It's up to you to choose your path.

Five things that make men fall

Last chapter I talked about the way of the prevailing man and the church. I gave you characteristics to grab onto that will help you advance your way through this world and into victory. Hopefully you understand by now that there is a war in this world and it is a spiritual war. There are good things to grab onto and there are bad. Since we are talking about the fall of mankind, I thought it was appropriate to give you five things in this world that can make a man fall. I pray you do not take these lightly. Men, there are so many things in this life that the enemy uses to destroy men of

God. I know there are many more than five but I tried to pick the top five that I believe have a large influence on us.

1) **Unbelief.** The first thing I think of when it comes to the word "unbelief," is when Jesus returned to His home town. Everywhere Jesus went miracles and signs followed. There is not a single time in the Bible that records Jesus refusing or denying anyone healing. Crowds and crowds of men and women flocked to Jesus to be healed, and He healed them ALL. It seemed that mighty works flowed from Him everywhere He went… except His own hometown. But why?

   Mark 6, verse 5 and 6 (NKJV) explain. *"Now He could do no mighty work there, except that He laid His hands on a few sick people and healed them. <u>And He marveled because of their unbelief.</u> Then He went about the villages in a circuit, teaching."* We are talking about the Son of God here, Jesus Christ Himself. The man who walked on water! God in the flesh! Why didn't He just heal everyone? Did He choose not to heal everyone? He always healed everyone before. What made this situation so different?

   The thing is, God manifests Himself through faith and belief in God, not unbelief. If you read earlier, the people in His hometown only recognized Him as Joseph and Mary's boy, the carpenter, but did not believe in Him as the Messiah. Their unbelief limited the power of God. I know, God is almighty and all powerful, but He is also a God of His word, and His word constantly tells us to, "have

faith," and "believe in the Son of Man." He commands
these multiple times throughout **John** and many other times
throughout the New Testament.

When we are acting in unbelief, we are not acting in
faith. Faith pleases God, not unbelief (see **Hebrews 11:6**).
If the enemy can get you to have a lack of faith, then he can
get you to fall. One of the biggest downfalls of men is a
lack of belief in the power of God. Much like the man with
leprosy in **Luke 5,** who said to Jesus, *"If you are willing,
you can heal me and make me clean,"* we tend to have the
same belief system. You see, this man knew Jesus could
heal him, but he wasn't sure if he was willing. Many
Christians believe that God can heal, but they do not have
faith that He is willing to heal. Jesus made it very clear here
that not only could He heal this man, but He was very
willing to do so, raising this man's faith.

Think about this: if Jesus was in front of you in the
flesh and said, "Go to the store and lay hands on a lady in
the bread isle and she will be healed." You probably would
have a great amount of faith due to the fact that our Lord
and Savior assured it would happen. He spoke it to you face
to face. This man was told by Jesus himself, *"I am willing.
Be clean!"* The man went away knowing that God did not
lack in power and did not lack in compassion. Belief in the
Son of God is powerful. Belief in Jesus Christ will change
your life. Unbelief steals, kills and destroys. God does not
lack in the power to answer prayer, but it's us who lack in
faith and dabble in unbelief.

2) **Strife**. I once heard a preacher say, "Strife is the manifestation of the enemy." I believe it's true. Strife is one of those things that destroys people and demolishes relationships, especially churches. If you do not know how to get rid of strife, you will end up defeated every single time.

I will give you an example. Leana and I had a lot to learn when it came to relationships. We clashed a lot and we let strife grow and grow, and when the harvest came, it was bad. It seemed like we were covered in gasoline and just a little hint of strife sparked an explosion. But that's what happens when we do not know how to defeat it. That's what happens when you let it linger. One small crack in a dam may not seem that bad, but give it time and the pressure of all that water will turn that small crack into a giant hole. Before you know it, the dam is gone and the water is destroying trees and landscapes all around.

James 3:16 (NKJV) says it best, *"For where envying and strife is, there is confusion and every evil work."* Strife is confusion. Strife is evil. Strife exists where there is chaos. And as the Bible says, *"God is not the author of confusion (chaos) but of peace,"* (**1 Corinthians 14:33 NKJV**). If not dealt with right away, strife can become the downfall of a man and everything he has in life. Men, do not let strife overcome you. *"Hatred stirs up strife, but love covers all sins."* (**Proverbs 10:12**).

3) **Fear**. Fear and unbelief kind of go hand-in-hand. Where there is fear, unbelief usually resides. The first thing that

popped in my mind was what kind of spirit God put in us. **2 Timothy 1:7** says, *"For God has not given us a spirit of fear, but of power and of love and of a sound mind."* I hear a lot of people say, "A little fear won't hurt anyone." They may be trying to comfort someone, but the thing is, fear is not of God. Reverent fear is different from the fear the enemy tries to instill in us. The truth is: fear can and will hurt someone. I know people whose fear has literally caused them to worry so much that they had heart attacks.

Most doctors will agree that stress and worry can literally kill you. Where does stress and anxiety come from? It is caused by fear. As a former EMT, I studied the anatomy and physiology of the body, and I realized that the body's chemical level can easily become uneven when you are worried and/or anxious. Fear just doesn't affect you physically, but spiritually as well. Fear paralyzes a Christian's faith walk. And according to **2 Timothy**, God did not give us a spirit that is of fear, but He gave us a spirit that gives us **power**, that gives of **love**, and gives of **soundness of mind**. Fear is a reason why many prayers go unanswered. Fear is the reason why many men of God fall. Fear is the reason why so many do not come to Jesus.

It reminds me of the story of Jairus, a ruler of the synagogue (see **Luke 8:40-54**). Jairus came to Jesus and fell at His feet and begged Him to come and heal his 12 year old daughter who was dying. Jesus began to set out to heal this little girl. Skip down to **verse 49**. While Jesus was speaking to someone else, someone from Jairus' house came and told him not to bother Jesus because his daughter had already died. This was a turning point for Jairus. He had a choice here to respond in faith or fear. I believe fear tried to creep in right away.

Can you imagine being told that? Can you imagine the thoughts that flooded his mind? In the natural realm of things, that's it, your daughter is dead. There is no turning back; it's too late. *"Hearing this, Jesus said to Jairus, 'Do not be afraid; just believe, and she will be healed.'"* (**Luke 8:50**). What was Jesus' answer to Jairus? He told him to get rid of fear; instead, to believe, and if he did this, his daughter will be healed. When you fear, you will get the things of fear, but when you have faith and believe, you will get the things of faith and belief: the manifestation of God's power and love.

Men, do not let fear enslave you. Do not let fear cripple you. Do not let fear be your demise. Much like the house of Jairus, many people will scoff and laugh at your faith. They laughed at Jesus' faith, but it didn't stop Jesus from grabbing Jairus' daughter by the hand and pulling her up, saying, *"My child, get up!"* Having faith in Jesus was the best decision Jairus had ever made, and I bet he was glad he didn't choose to fear. The decision between fear and faith could cost you something great in your life.

4) **Lying**. Out of the six things that God hates (see **Proverbs 6:16-19**), lying has to do with about three-fourths of them. Lying is one of those things that start off as a "not a big deal" type of thing, but can so easily become a huge problem. You would be surprised about how many times

we actually lie in a day. Whether it is joking or just flat out lying to someone, we do it a lot. Some people exaggerate stories, others lie out of fear, and many do it on purpose to hurt people.

#DearChristianMen, there is never ever a good reason to lie. Why? Because God does not lie. He never lied and He never will lie. Lying is of the devil. It really is. *"You belong to your father, the devil, and you want to carry out your father's desires. He was a murderer from the beginning, not holding to the truth, for there is no truth in him. When he lies, he speaks his native language, for he is a liar and the father of lies,"* (**John 8:44**).

I am not calling you children of the devil, men. But if you are constantly lying, you are showing characteristics of the devil. Lying is not a characteristic of God. It is nothing even close to God, so why show it or act in that manner? Lying is like opening all the doors in your home and hoping a thief doesn't get in and rob you blind.

One thing you should get in your mind is the fact that God knows the truth. You can't lie to God and get away with it. You may be able to lie to others and cover up your secrets; you may even be able to lie to yourself, but the truth will be uncovered. I remember I used to lie out of fear. Back in the day, when I was at work and I would mess up on something, I would lie to try and make it so it didn't look like my fault. It was a terrible choice. A majority of the time I was just digging myself deeper into a hole. Lying always made things worse.

I say this from the bottom of my heart, men, please strive to be a truthful man of God. There is nothing more unattractive than a man that you can't trust. Even if it hurts to tell the truth, do it. Even if telling the truth will get you fired, do it anyway and I promise you will never regret it.

Quick story time. When I was in high school, my friends and I were hanging out in the band hallway. As I opened my bag, I found a glass stink bomb in there from a previous camping trip (don't ask). You know those stink bombs, right? They are glass and have a yellow liquid in them and if you break the glass it smells like someone lit a giant pile of trash and hair on fire. Yea, that kind. Well, I went to hand it to my friend who had is hand out and at the last second he moved it and I dropped it on the ground. The whole hallway began to smell extremely bad in seconds. All four of us took off and got out of there, but unfortunately many people noticed us leaving. The principle called us all in the office separately. Me being the fine young man I am, decided to lie, thinking my friends would all tell the same story. Well, I was the only one who lied, making me look like a fool. It was because I was a fool. I got in trouble, not because of the stink bomb, but because I lied. You know, people respect honesty, even when you are guilty. Man up and tell the truth, ALWAYS.

5) **Pride**. This is probably the biggest reason men of God fall. It's probably one of the biggest reasons why men never step up either. My pastor once said, "Satan will try and hold you back in fear and false humility, but he will just as

easy let go of you and have you fall flat on your face in pride too." In other words, when we realize all the things God has done for us, there is the temptation to get prideful too. Which is why so many men fall flat on their faces.

What was the reason why Satan rebelled in the first place? Pride. He became prideful and wanted to be God. **Ezekiel 28:13** and **14** tells us that Satan was covered in every precious stone imagined and he was called the "anointed cherub." He was "the model of perfection, full of wisdom and perfect in beauty (see **Ezekiel 28:14**). Some say he was the highest of all angels. I mean, he must have been persuasive enough to convince one-third of the angels to rebel with him (see **Revelation 12:14**), right? Satan fell because of pride. He did not like being second best. He wanted to be God (see **Isaiah 14:13**). He was created by God so he had to be great, but it went to his head and he thought he was greater than the creator.

Humility is one of the keys to success in God's eyes. Just as pride was the fall of Satan and his angels, pride will be the fall of you if you choose so. Men, be on your guard when it comes to success. Give God all the glory. A humble heart is the main weapon against pride. *God opposes the proud, but gives grace to the humble* (**James 4:6 ESV**). *For everyone who exalts himself will be humbled, and he who humbles himself will be exalted* (**Luke 14:11 ESV**). *The reward for humility and fear of the Lord is riches and honor and life* (**Proverbs 22:4 ESV**). *Do nothing from rivalry or conceit, but in humility count others more significant than yourselves. Let each of* *you look not only to his own interests, but also to the interests of others. Have this mind among yourselves, which is yours in Christ Jesus, who, though he was in the form of God, did not count equality with God a thing to be grasped, but made himself nothing, taking the form of a servant, being born in the likeness of men* (**Philippians 2 ESV**).

Stay in HIM

#DearChristianMen, your success will always and only be in God. Anything outside that will be your death; spiritually and/or physically. Do not be afraid to fall, instead be determined to rise up. Be on your guard, men, and never fear the enemy, for if you are truly in God, you are more than a conqueror.

"Watch, stand fast in the faith, be brave, be strong. Let all that you do be done with love," (**1 Corinthians 16:13-14 NKJV**).

"So then, just as you received Christ Jesus as Lord, continue to live in him, rooted and but up in him, strengthened in the faith as you were taught, and overflowing with thankfulness (**Colossians 2: 6,7**). *"*

#DEARCHRISTIANMEN

9

THE RIGHTEOUS MAN

Are you a sinner or a saint?

#DearChristianMen, this is such an important question to ask yourselves. Am I just a sinner saved by grace? Or am I considered a saint? I hear many Christians argue both sides. In all honesty, it doesn't matter what anyone's opinion is on this topic, what does the Bible say about you as a child of God? That is the real question. Here's the problem: if you see yourself as a dirty old sinner who has just been forgiven, then it's really going to hinder you from receiving everything God wants you to have.

Let's say you were a street bum. Everyone around you always told you that you were a street bum, so you acted like a bum, talked like a bum and lived like a bum. One day you inherit a kingdom, but no one ever tells you. It's yours and that title belongs to you now, but you are still living as a street bum because you were never shown what really belonged to you. That's what is happening in the body of Christ today. We were broken and dirty people before we accepted Jesus in to our hearts. We were sinners on our way to hell. But we have been made new, from rags to riches, yet people are still teaching that we are filthy rags before the Lord.

Men, this is not to boast on anything we have done because it was all Christ, but we have inherited a Kingdom and we have been redeemed and made royalty. We have become saints. And the best part is: we have become right standing with God (which is what righteous means). Calling ourselves sinners and worthless can sound humble, but there is nothing humbling about it. It's a false humility and it has deceived millions of Christians. The Bible didn't even call the church at Corinth forgiven sinners, but Paul referred to them as saints, and that was the most sinful church in the early church. They were praying in tongues, yet were having orgies in the church and taking part in sexual immorality. Yet they were still known as saints according to God's Word!

God's Word is clear that our old sinful man has died (see **Romans 6:11**) and was buried with Christ (see **Romans 6:2, 4**), and we are new creatures in Christ Jesus (See **2 Corinthians 5:17**). The sin needs to go, yes, and I am not condoning the sins of Corinth, but I am just making a point so you can understand that just because we sin, does not make us dirty sinners. If by "sinner" you mean someone who still sins, then yes, I guess you can call us sinners, but the Bible doesn't even refer to a believer as a "sinner." Everything that labeled us a sinner before we were saved has been put to death. That is not our nature any more.

In **Colossians 3:5**, Paul tells us, *"Put to death, therefore, whatever belongs to your earthly nature: sexual immorality, impurity, lust, evil desires and greed, which is idolatry. Because of these, the wrath of God is coming. You used to walk in these ways, in the life you once lived. But now you must rid yourselves of all such things as these: anger, rage, malice, slander, and filthy language from your lips. Do not lie to each other, since you have taken off your old self with its practices and have put on the new self, which is being renewed in the knowledge in the image of its Creator."*

We literally go from death to life. We have been crucified with Christ (see **Romans 6:2-13; 7:4-6; 2 Corinthians 5:14; Galatians 2:20; 5:24; 6:14; Colossians 2:20; 3:3-5; 1 Peter 2:24**), Our old sinner nature died with Christ on the cross(see **Romans 6:6; 7:4-6; Colossians 3:9, 10**), and Christ's resurrection guarantees our new life not only now, but eternally with God in Heaven forever (see **Romans 6:4, 11; Colossians 2:12, 13; 3:1, 3**).

Definition of "sinner"

If you look up the word sinner in the New Testament Greek, you'll find the Greek word *hamartolos*, which means: *one devoted to sin, a sinner; not free from sin; pre-eminently sinful, especially wicked; all wicked men, specifically of men stained with certain definitive vices or crimes; tax collectors, heathens, etc.*[6] So according to this definition, if you believe we are just forgiven sinners then you must believe we are a people forgiven but STILL in bondage to sin. Right? Yes? No? So here is the real question: are we still in bondage to sin? Here is a better question: are YOU still in bondage to sin?

There is an instance where Jesus was speaking in **John 8:31-36** about believers who were in bondage to sin, but it was bondage due to ignorance. But men, this is not who we were called to be. Did Jesus set you free by his death and resurrection? If you answered yes (which he did) then the truth of **verse 36** is more powerful than you have ever seen it: *"So if the Son sets you free, you will be free indeed."* Jesus freed us from this lifestyle of sin, but you can so easily stay a slave to sin if you want. No really, He lets you choose. Sad part is, there is not much power to overcome taught in churches now days. I have been in a lot of churches and talked to a lot of Christians and not many talk with confidence that they are truly freed. There is a lot of murmuring and complaining. There are many Christians giving into bondage because they just don't have an understanding of the freedom that has been offered to them. Men, we have been freed but it's our choice to choose to walk in that freedom from the bondage of sin.

Question time!

Now, in order to really make you think, I want to ask you some questions. I took the definition of "sinner" and put it in question form. After asking myself these questions I really saw things in a different light. These really challenged me and helped me to see myself in the light of Christ.

1) Would you consider yourself a forgiven man who is still devoted to sin?
2) Would you consider yourself somebody who is forgiven, but not freed from sin?
3) Would you consider yourself someone who is forgiven but especially wicked?
4) Would you consider yourself a forgiven wicked person?
5) Would you consider yourself a forgiven heathen?

By now, I pray you are really thinking about where you stand as a believer. If we take what I just asked you, you start to see things a little differently I hope. You start to see that a forgiven "sinner" by this definition is someone who is forgiven but is not necessarily free. He is still in bondage and needing freed from sin.

The thing we have to understand is that Jesus didn't die to just forgive us; He died to free us. He took our sins and destroyed any power they had over us. If He did only die to forgive us then we can probably label ourselves as forgiven sinners, but that's not what happened. Jesus didn't just *cover* our sins; the Bible tells us he *became* our sins. He freed us from our chains and we were given the chance to be free from the slavery and bondage of sin.

I don't know about you, but when I read the Bible I see myself as a brand new creation in Christ Jesus. I see that my old 'sinner' self is dead and long gone (see **Romans 6:11**). I see that my old self was buried with Christ, no longer to define who I am (see **Romans 6:2, 4**). And I am a brand new man in Christ Jesus (see **2 Corinthians 5:17**)! Isn't this the gospel we are called to preach? A gospel of reconciliation? A gospel of restoration? A gospel of complete redemption, not partial redemption?

So… am I a saint?

So if you are not labeled a sinner, then does that mean we are saints? Yes it does! A lot of people hear the word "saint" and automatically think of someone high above the rest. Being a saint is nothing to boast about because, like I said before, the only reason any of us have become forgiven and right standing with God is all glory to Jesus Christ! We were nothing without Christ.

The word "saint" actually means somebody who is holy[7], and we have been made holy with the righteousness of God through, and only through, the bloodshed of Christ Jesus! **2 Corinthians 5:21** tells us, "*God made him who had no sin to be sin for us, so that in him we might become the righteousness of God.*" To clarify, Paul starts off his letter to the Corinthians with this: "*Unto the church of God which is at Corinth, to them that are sanctified in Christ Jesus, called to be saints, with all that in every place call upon the name of Jesus Christ our Lord, both theirs and ours: (KJV)*"

He was writing to everyone in Corinth who has asked Jesus to be their Lord and Savior, and called them saints. He even referred to them as "saints" after chapter 5, which is where he addressed their sexual sins. Paul chewed these guys out. They were bragging about their sexual immorality and Paul had to set them straight. But let's not lose focus of the message Paul is trying to get by them.

The message of Corinthians shows that a saint is not somebody who is perfect by the things they have done in life. A saint is somebody who's been made perfect, forgiven and redeemed, through the blood of Jesus Christ. Are you starting to see the whole theme of Christianity now? All these amazing things have been given to us by Christ Jesus. They all are things we did not deserve but He gave them to us anyway because He loved us. Just because we didn't deserve it, doesn't mean that it's not true. It's who we are now. It's what we have been transformed into.

Our sins are forgiven forever! Am I telling you it's ok to abuse God's grace? By no means! Knowing that you are a saint through Jesus Christ's sacrifice should make you want to live a holy life. It's not a credit card to sin, but an empowerment to change into the men God is calling you to be. His love and compassion should lead us to repentance and a complete life change. None of this is to boast in anything we have done. It's all glory to Jesus Christ. If only we can truly grasp all that He went through for us to have.

Breaking the chains of sin

Even though Jesus has set us free from the bondage of sin, there are still many Christians who have not yet grasped the true power of Christ's death and resurrection. It is honestly just a lack of being taught, or being taught the wrong thing. Jesus speaks of this in **John 8:31-36**: *"To the Jews who had believed him, Jesus said, 'If you hold to my teaching, you are really my disciples. Then you will know the truth and the truth will set you free.' They answered him, 'We are Abraham's descendants and have never been slaves of anyone. How can you say that we shall be set free?' Jesus replied, 'I tell you the truth, everyone who sins is a slave to sin. Now a slave has no permanent place in the family, but a son belongs to it forever. So if the Son sets you free, you will be free indeed."*

I want you to get this, men: The more we become aware of the goodness and the love of God, the more we will be able to love Him. That understanding will spark a hatred towards sin. The more we become like Him, the more we start to love the things He loves and hate the things He hates. After all, the Bible does tell us that the goodness of God leads to repentance, right? **Romans 2:4**, *"Or do you show contempt for the riches of his kindness, forbearance and patience, not realizing that God's kindness is intended to lead you to repentance?"*

Once you begin to grab a hold of the God's goodness, your love for Him will begin to grow and mature beyond anything you could ever imagine. Like I said before, His love changes things. His love changes people. His love causes our love to grow and expand (see **1 John 4:19**). We soon find ourselves able to love others better than we thought we could. Before I found Christ, I thought I did a good job of loving people. But with Christ, my love for others become so much more pure and passionate.

Men, when you let God fully into your life, His love starts a chain reaction of transformation. When our love increases for others and especially for Him, we will begin to naturally desire to keep Jesus' commandments as Jesus himself said in **John 14:23**, "Jesus replied, '*If anyone loves me, he will obey my teaching. My Father will love him, and we will come to him and make our home with him.*'"

To many, this may start to sound confusing. Bear with me, men. Keep reading these scriptures over and over again. As we grow in love for God, our love for others will grow naturally as well (see **1 John 5:1**). Jesus explained it like this: If we love God with everything we have, and love our neighbors as Christ has loved us, we fulfill all the law (see **Matthew 22:37-40**).

Let me paint you a picture. You have a clothes line. One pole is your love for God. The other pole is your love for others. A wire connects the two. Hooked on this wire are all the laws, or you can say, all of Jesus' commands he gave us. These two love commands hold up all those laws, but when one of those posts become week, the wire becomes lose and starts to fall. If we stop loving God with everything we have, that becomes a problem. If we stop loving others as Jesus loves us, that becomes a problem as well. As long as we are fulfilling these two commands, we fulfill everything. When we love others and love God, we will not want to covet our neighbor's wife, we will not want to steal, we will not want to murder, and we will not want to dishonor our parents or any other command. Love is a powerful thing. Love will cause us to overcome sin. Love is the weapon against breaking the bondage of sin. Love never failed anyone and it never will. God's love is the key to all your problems.

Growing up in Christ

Meditating on God's Word and learning of God's goodness is extremely powerful when it comes to tearing down strongholds (incorrect ways of thinking based on lies and deception). Just like any other man of God in the Bible, I believe with all my heart that the reason King David developed a very deep and intimate relationship with God was because he actually spent time with Him. He messed up a lot, but David took time to seek God and talk with Him. God was not just some foreign being or idea to Him, He was His everything; his life source. David had a very intimate relationship with God and we can have that same relationship.

#DearChristianMen, knowing (realizing) the love of Christ allows us to be filled with the fullness of God. **Ephesians 3:19**, "*and to know this love that surpasses knowledge—that you may be filled to the measure of all the* *fullness of God."* Knowing the love of God will help us to grow up in Christ (see **Ephesians 4:13**).

Men, this is what being a man of God is all about; grabbing hold of the power of God. Looking down on yourself and thinking that you are a dirty old sinner never made anyone into a man. In fact, it has only made passive men who do not step up into their roles as leaders. Growing up in Christ has a lot to do with walking and talking in love, just like Jesus. The way we talk and act is a key sign of whether we are mature in Christ or just baby Christians. As every child must do, it's time to grow up. And it starts with talking and walking in love.

I know it seems like I am beating this into your head, but this is something that so many Christians miss. This is very important, men. Sometimes it takes hearing something a hundred times before finally understanding it.

How do I keep my way pure?

Like I said before, it's easy for us to get on fire for God, but the part many men struggle with is *staying* on fire for Him. There are churches today that are good at telling men that they are not pure and that what they are doing is wrong, but they do not equip and teach them how to get out of sin and stay out of it. The thing is, most of us know what we are doing is not the best, but no one trains us up. Nobody provides a way for us to get out of the lifestyle we are in and into a greater purpose.

This is the biggest reason I am writing this book: to educate you and equip you. Do I have it all together? No, I do not. I have a long ways to go. But the reason I was able to grow and mature in the Lord was because I had an awesome group of men after God's heart that showed me what a real man was all about. The life they lived in church in front of everyone was the same exact life they lived outside those walls. I saw the way they respected their wives and treated them like queens. And the women honored them because the men were so lost in God's love that they knew how to love their woman. They were bold, yet so gentle. They submitted to authority and served with passion. They were funny, but appropriate. They spoke with words of encouragement and saw people through eyes of grace. They never once boasted in themselves, but always gave God the glory.

I witnessed this first hand and it opened my eyes. I was not only taught how to be a man; I was shown real life examples. The church does not need more boys, we need more men. God does not need Christians half way in and half way out; He needs men who are completely sold out for God. He needs men who have chosen the road marked "holy" and "pure." But CJ, how do we do that? How can I keep my ways pure? How can I be a better man and stay that way? I'm glad you asked! This is what God says about it.

"How can a young man keep his way pure? By living according to your word. I seek you with all my heart; do

not let me stray from your commands. I have hidden your word in my heart that I may not sin against you. Praise be to you, O Lord; teach me your decrees. With my lips I recount all the laws that come from your mouth. I rejoice in following your statutes as one rejoices in great riches. I meditate on your precepts and consider your ways. I delight in your decrees; I will not neglect your word," – **Psalm 119:9-16**.

When I read **Psalm 119** I see such passion and reverence for God's word. I see a man writing about something he is completely consumed by. The words come to life and become an outline for Christians everywhere, especially men. Some suggest that the author of this Psalm was Ezra the High Priest, but whether it was him or David or another man of God, one thing remains true: there is something captivating about God's Word.

This world is drowning in a sea of sexual images and sinful attractions. Everywhere we go, we find temptation that so easily entangle us and pulls us away from the source of true life. The writer asks the question that every man once asked themselves: How can we stay pure in such a wicked world?

#DearChristianMen, we cannot do this on our own. We need the strength and wisdom that comes from God alone. These eight versus give us an outline that shows us exactly how to stay pure. Men, there are no shortcuts in our faith walk. We will not wake up tomorrow arriving at perfection.

Below I broke down **Psalm 119:9-16** for you.

1) Live out what God's word says!
2) Seek God with everything you have.
3) Do not stray away from His Word.
4) Hide His words in your heart; store them up and protect them.
5) Ask God to show you His ways.
6) Confess out loud the Word of God!
7) Rejoice and be thankful in EVERYTHING!
8) Meditate on what He asks of us.
9) Delight in God's goodness and love.
10) Do not neglect His word.

It's kind of weird because in Chapter Two I said that there is no "'10 Step Guide to Getting Your MAN OF GOD Badge," but clearly I just marked out ten things that can keep a man from stumbling. Just go with it, haha! But on a serious note, these verses give us an idea of how to stay pure in a wicked world. Teach these to your spouse, your kids, your friends and your family. Write them down, put them in your phone and make reminders. Do whatever it takes to remind yourself of these life changing guidelines.

Obviously for the author, these words changed his life and opened his eyes to true living for God. They were words he needed to write down to tell the world and anyone else who read this. These are words worthy to remember; worthy to keep in your heart.

The power of the cross and the victory of His resurrection

My pastor once told me, "When we think of the Gospel, we should think of one word: Exchange." When we think of what Jesus did for us on the cross, He made an exchange: our punishment for His righteousness. Jesus took everything we deserved when he died, and in exchange, he gave us his right standing with God. This knowledge right here will give us victory over condemnation.

You see men, when we doubt or struggle with our identity, many people say to look at the cross. They are right, what Jesus did on the cross was life-changing, but for me, I look past the cross and look to his resurrection. The resurrection has become more meaningful than it ever has before. Let me explain. Have you ever seen Mel Gibson's film, *The Passion of the Christ*? This movie does an amazing job at deeply touching us by Jesus' pain and suffering on the cross, but the thing is, we are not completely shown the power of His resurrection. We must appreciate the great price Jesus paid for our debt to sin, but the gospel should not end at his death. That was just the beginning. Jesus' death on the cross took our sin, but His resurrection conquered it. Without his resurrection, Jesus' ministry was in vain and our devotion would mean nothing. If we only dwell on his crucifixion, then we will miss the power of His resurrection.

I have seen many pictures and necklaces of Jesus still hanging on the cross; broken and beaten. Many of us still see Jesus like that today. We see Him broken and suffering; not being able to help us. And that is exactly where the Devil wants Him to stay. If Satan can keep us in that mindset, then we will never hope and believe for more.

You see, men, Jesus' suffering was a brief humiliation in order to bring greater glory. You know what that greater glory was? Do you know what joy Jesus saw in the cross? He saw you. He saw you redeemed and COMPLETELY transformed. He saw you no longer as a dirty sinner, but as a man made righteous before the Lord. If only we saw ourselves as God truly sees us now.

10

FINAL WORDS

Lost in the comfort zone

I remember a lady in my church that would always come alone. Over time, I got to know her and discovered just how wonderful of a woman of God she was. But something always bothered me: where was her husband?

One night after worship service, we were all just sitting around talking and I had a chance to sit down with her and chat. She then opened up about her husband. She explained to me how he was a Christian but he refused to come to our church. At first I was like, "Oh no, was it something we said? Was it something we did?" She explained to me that it was something that our church did: we challenged him… and he didn't want that. He wanted to stay at his other church. A church that let him feel comfortable about his life; a church that didn't push him to be more like Christ. He was lost in his comfort zone and did not have any urge to leave.

She was a strong woman of God, but I could see in

her eyes that she was missing something: her leader. Her husband was called to set the pace of their walk, but he was only slowing her down. Gradually she kept moving forward but he was lagging behind. She loved him so much, and I could tell she was hurting inside for her husband to lead her, but she was not giving up.

#DearChristianMen, this is happening more often than you realize. It's a plague that has hindered Christian relationships since the beginning and it has only grown since then. Women everywhere are flocking to church and seeking God more than ever, but their husbands are nowhere to be found. Pride, selfishness, laziness; call it what you want, but this one thing is true: Christian men are not stepping up, leaving their spouse to take on a position that they were never meant to take on.

Where are all the men?

This movement has raised a question: "Where are the men of God?" There is a hunger for leadership among the Body of Christ. Women and children everywhere desire leadership, integrity, passion, and humility. They are praying for men to step up, but so many do not grab hold of the calling. Women are wondering if they will ever find a true man of God. Churches are seeking more leaders to help out. Whether you see it or not, there is a serious lack of leaders in the Church, preferably men.

I remember at my old church they would put on

men and women conferences every so often. I would be called to usher at the women's conference and wow, they were always jam-packed! Women were everywhere and they were seeking the Lord with all they had. But the men's conferences were not nearly as filled. I would see men just standing there during worship or looking around during prayer. There was hardly any excitement on their faces. There was no outward expression of Christ in them, nor any desire to find it. The question was raised again: "Where are all these men of God?"

Everywhere I went I remember hearing story after story of these boys and girls growing up without a father figure in the home. There were even some families where the father was present, but he never led his family closer to Christ. Their wives would worship with everything they had, but the men would sit there with their hands in their pockets, barely moving.

I remember an instance like this one night as Leana and I went to a worship concert at a church in Elkhorn, NE. There was a couple in front of us. They looked like they were in their late 20's or early 30's. The woman was dancing and clapping her hands. You could tell she wanted to break out. Every so often I would notice that she would glance over at her husband who had his hands in his pockets and her dancing would slow down and her clapping would stop. It's like she was looking over to see her man worshipping God, and when he wasn't, she felt like maybe she was too much. I am not sure what was going through their minds, but one thing is for sure, when the man doesn't step up and out with love and passion for God, it effects people around you.

I have seen men encourage a large crowd with his worship, and I have seen men kill the mood. Should our heart for God be effected by others? No, but sometimes it just is. Sometimes it's hard to be the only one following God while those you love are not. It reminded me of many churches today. Men, being a leader is more than just being present. We need to guide, lead, equip and obey. We need to set the example. Being present is one thing, but actually leading is another. Men are present in the church, but there is no active leading. There are very few examples being set. And I don't mean to sound like a Negative Nancy, but there is a serious epidemic in the Body of Christ. We have gotten things backwards.

Deny self, gain abundant life

I believe one of the problems that men face when making the decision to go all in for God is that we tend to only see the things we have to give up in life instead of all the things we will receive from Christ. We can't live for the world and live for Christ at the same time; it's either one or the other. Sadly, most men think that living any other lifestyle than the one Christ offers is freedom, but in reality they are not free at all; they are slaves to their own laziness and sin. They become slaves to pride and man-made wisdom.

So many non-Christians, and even Christians, think that submission to God chains you down, but in reality, you become more free than you have ever been. In **John 8** Jesus just gets done explaining to a group of Jews that those who hold to his teachings will know the truth and the truth will set them free. They were confused because they didn't see themselves as slaves to anything. Jesus hits them with a bold statement in **verse 34**, *"Very truly I tell you, everyone who sins is a slave to sin."*

To many men (and women), this is where they are. They think they are free but they do not see their spiritual chains. They are blind to their bondage and yet promise others freedom, while they themselves are slaves of depravity--for "people are slaves to whatever has mastered them," (see **2 Peter 2:19**). This is where these Jews were at. They had no idea that their self-righteous and religious living meant nothing to God unless their hearts were on fire for Him. But Jesus gives them hope in **verse 36** when he says, *"So if the Son sets you free, you will be free indeed."*

Men, you have to understand something about God; when He does something, he really does do it. He doesn't kind of do it, He doesn't sort of do it, and He doesn't do it at poor quality. God is not quantity over quality; He gets it completely done at the best time, at the best quality, and the best way possible. When God heals you, you are HEALED. When God saves you, you are SAVED. And when God sets you free, you are completely FREE. No "ifs" "ands" or "buts" about it. Whether you see it, feel it, or don't believe it at all, everything you need to live a godly life has been bought and paid for by the blood of Jesus Christ.

Submitting to God is not slavery. Submitting to God is freedom you have never experienced before. Can you imagine not worrying about the cares of this world? Can you imagine having a constant joy deep down that nothing can shake? Can you imagine having a peace that surpasses all understanding? Can you imagine worshipping God freely without worry or fear of what others think about you? THAT'S real freedom. No fear, no worry, no frustrations. And it's available for any believer. It's available for YOU.

High expectations and misplaced worship

When I first became a Christian, I thought that every man that went to church was on fire for God. I was so wrong. It was not long after that, that I discovered there was a real lack of men on fire for God. Yes, there were always men in the church, but now that I look back, there was no real excitement for God among these men. They came, punched their church time card, and then left in time to catch the kick-off of their football team. Where were the men?

They were at work, they were watching or attending their favorite sports games, they were hunting, they were in front of a video game screen, and they were in places they shouldn't be. They were so dedicated to the "things" and "stuff" of this world that they lost focus of the reason for life: To love the Lord your God with all your heart and with all your soul and with all your strength and with all your mind (see **Luke 10:27; Matthew 22:37; Mark 12:30; Deuteronomy 6:5**). Their heart, soul, strength, and mind were all in the wrong place. They were worshipping created things instead of the Creator. To them, church was just a thing you do because you're a Christian. To them, God was too distant to even have a relationship with. To them, sports, hunting, work, and video games were more real than a fellowship with our Creator.

It's sad, it really is, but it's true. Imagine if men looked forward to spending time with God like they look forward to going to play basketball, or workout, or go to a sports game. What would it be like if the zeal we had for cars was the same as we had for God? Or if we pursued God like we pursued women. Makes you think, huh?

The more you know, the more you understand you don't really know much

I told you before and I am not afraid to say it a thousand more times: I am not perfect, not even close, but I praise God I am not where I used to be. When I first decided to follow Jesus with everything I had, I thought I was a man. I was only 20 years old and I felt like I was mature and understood a lot about being an adult. I was completely wrong. I was nowhere close. The more I learned about becoming a man of God, the more I realized how much I really didn't know.

I am convinced that the Holy Spirit can and will teach us all things if we let Him. But I also know that we can learn a great deal from our mistakes as well. Is that the route I prefer? No, but it happened and I praise God for guiding me through those times. I made a lot of mistakes along the way. God's word taught me a lot about what it means to become a real man, but I learned quite a few things from my mess ups as well. The moment we start to think we know everything is the moment we become deceived by the devil. Sometimes too much knowledge can be a bad thing.

Let me explain. Solomon asked for wisdom above all else and God was pleased with Him (see **2 Chronicles 1**). Solomon wanted wisdom to lead God's people, not just to look good or feel good. Wisdom and knowledge from God is a great thing. It's something we all should desire. But knowledge without God supplying it can be empty and worthless. Sometimes we can fill ourselves up with facts and info about the Bible and God, but that's all it becomes, just facts. There is no encounter with God. There is no power to it. There is no faith involved. We began to think with logic more than with faith. The promises of God become harder and harder to believe. We over analyze and overthink, leaving us drained.

In an era where we have vast amounts of knowledge at the tip of our fingers, we have literally overheated our brains with mere knowledge of the bible and lost touch with the simple things of Christianity. You may be able to memorize the whole Bible, you may even be able to shoot off quotes, cliché comments, and sound like a Christian, but without a personal relationship with God, it means nothing. You just become fat off of knowledge. You can have all the wisdom and knowledge of the world, but without God at the center of your life, it means absolutely nothing.

The blood of Jesus Christ

There was a time when there existed some strife between my fiancé and me. As any relationship goes, things happen and selfishness seeps in between two people and causes friction. There was definitely some annoyance going on between each other. At the time we were just engaged so I left her house without saying much, but in my mind I was confused and angry all at the same time. I wanted her to see things my way. To me, I felt like I was in the right and she was hurting me. In other words, I was tired of doing good.

You see, men, the Bible tells us that true love never tires of doing good. **1 Corinthians 13** tells us what real love looks like: *"Love is patient, love is kind. It does not envy, it does not boast, it is not proud. It is not rude, it is not self-seeking, it is not easily angered, it keeps no record of wrongs. Love does not delight in evil but rejoices with the truth. It always protects, always trusts, always hopes, always perseveres."*

Men, there will be people out there who may not

love you the way you want them to or the way they should, but it doesn't matter. Real love is not self-seeking. Real love loves and never stops loving. Real love is patient through the toughest storms. As for me, well, I lost focus of what real love was that night when I left without even saying "I love you."

When I got home, I began to do the dishes. My roommate, and best bro, could tell something was on my mind. As I had my hand inside one of the glasses, my mind was racing with frustration. Suddenly, the glass broke in my hand. I just sat there, trying not to get angry. As I looked down, I noticed my knuckle was bleeding pretty good. My roommate gave me a napkin and I began to wipe the blood up. My roommate walked away and said, "You know, it doesn't go unnoticed."

Just then, I looked down at the blood covered napkin and immediately thought of Jesus and his death on the cross. The blood on my napkin seemed like a lot, but Jesus shed way more blood for us, and you know who he did it for? Not only you and I, who would accept him, but he even did it for those who would never accept him or love him.

He gave his life, the greatest act of love, for those who would show him no love, but Jesus never tired of doing good. For the joy set before him, He went to the cross (see **Hebrews 12:2**), but why? Because He loved you and I. Not with just any ordinary love, but perfect love; a love that never gave up; a love that stayed patient; a love that never tired of doing good for his creation. He gave up his entire life for me, and here I was pouting while doing dishes.

If anyone had the right to be angry, it was Jesus. The King of kings and the Lord of lords came down from His throne to reconcile us, and those who were "godly" rejected him: sending Him to the cross to die the worst death known to man at that time. He shed His blood at the whipping post, He shed his blood carrying the cross, and whatever He had left, He gave it all up for us on Calgary Hill. He bled from his head where a crown of thorns was not just placed, but forced on. He bled from His back, sides, and front at the whipping post, while His flesh was being ripped from His body. He bled from His feet and hands where the nails were hammered into Him. And He bled from His side where He was pierced by the spear. If you look at the whole picture, Jesus bled all He could bleed. Every last drop was given during His crucifixion.

All of that for me? All of that for us? I admit, I broke down and cried. How could I be so selfish after everything Jesus had done for me? You and I, we can never tire of doing good. Not after the death that Christ died for us; not after everything He died to give us. Not after all the blood He shed for us: that perfect and spotless blood. That, my friends, is true love. A love that never holds back any good thing.

A casual Christianity

In the Old Testament, following God was not a casual thing like many Christians make it today. Many Christians pray casually, go to church casually, and live their lives casually towards God. To them, God's presence is nothing to reverence, as if it is no big deal the things that God has done through Jesus Christ. Men, we have to get this. We have to understand this. This is powerful. We, as believers in the new covenant, have an amazing gift. When we accept Jesus as our Lord and Savior, the Bible tells us that God's Spirit dwells in us now. It's something that many of us take lightly. God's presence…. Lives inside of every believer now. God himself dwells in us. Think about this. This is something that truly needs to be grasped.

In the Old Testament, God's presence was something serious. God didn't just reveal himself to anybody and everybody. His presence was epic. Back then, God's presence dwelled in the temple in an area called the Holy of Holies. The High Priest was only allowed to go in once a year and in order to do so he had to be ceremonially cleansed. If he wasn't, the high priest would drop dead where he stood. That's how powerful and fearful God's presence was.

Back then, God dwelling with humans was not something easily grasped. Even after building the temple, Solomon said, "*But will God really dwell on earth? The heavens, even the highest heaven, cannot contain you. How much less this temple I have built!*" (**1 Kings 8:27, 2**

Chron. 2:6, 6:18). Solomon knew how great and amazing God's presence was, yet he could not even fathom the idea that God would choose the temple he built to dwell in here on earth. God's presence was not to be taken lightly. Honor and respect was the foundation of their faith.

Let me ask you something. When you hear the word "salvation" what do you automatically think of? Many of us immediately think of the forgiveness of sins. When we hear "eternal life" we think of heaven. We think of living forever. We think of life after this one. But you want to hear something crazy? That's not what eternal life is. In **John 3:16** Jesus says, *"For God so loved the world that He gave his only begotten son that whoever believes in him will not perish but have eternal life."*

It's easy to grab hold of the part where it says, "will not perish." That's awesome! Forgiveness of sins allows us to go to heaven! Praise God! But honestly, forgiveness of sins is just the beginning of eternal life. It's an opening to eternal life. Jesus didn't come to just forgive us, he came to give us eternal life. Sin separated us from God, so Jesus had to come down and deal with sin. However, His payment for sin was just a step toward His ultimate purpose of reconciling man to God.

If someone believes that Jesus died for their sins but doesn't go on to enter into a close relationship with God, then they are missing eternal life! So what is eternal life then? Eternal life is not a length of life. In fact, it is a quality of life. Eternal life is intimacy with the Father and

Jesus. In **John 17:3**, Jesus reveals to us what eternal life really is. He says, *"Now this is eternal life: that they know you, the only true God, and Jesus Christ, whom you have sent."*

There are many people who have been deceived without even realizing it. They are being told that Jesus came to forgive us of our sins and that's it. Even if that was all that He did for us, it would have been wonderful and quite frankly, much more than we deserved, but much less than what He actually accomplished for us.

It's a religion about a relationship

It sounds cliché, and you have probably heard it a million times, but Christianity is truly about a relationship with God. It's what eternal life is. It's the whole reason God sent Jesus. It's the meaning of life. Which is why we cannot take Christianity casually. "Why are you so extreme about this whole Jesus thing?" Because what Jesus did for me was extreme. What he did for me was far from casual. What He gave me in return was not something to take lightly.

This is not some fairytale and a goody-good, feel-good trip. Men, this is vital. We need to see this and understand it. Without true honor and reverence towards God, our Christianity is powerless. Our Christianity may not even be genuine. Our Christianity may not even be Christianity without a true and intimate friendship with our

Savior. Without that relationship, life is pointless. Christianity without Christ is just "ianity," and that means nothing… it literally means nothing [insert laughter here].

Final, final words

#DearChristianMen, it's been a blast writing this book. I don't want you going away thinking that I have it all together, because I don't. Maybe you don't think that, but then again, maybe you do. For me, I saw authors and pastors as men and women who had it all together. Why else would they write a book, right? But it's not that at all. One night during church my pastor was completely real with us, telling us about his struggles and his thoughts on certain situations. He was completely transparent, and that blessed me more than a thousand sermons put together; to know that I wasn't the only one in the world who thought like that, who doubted sometimes, who struggled with faith, and who got lazy.

These pastors, authors, and speakers, they were just teaching others the things they have learned over the years with the sole purpose of helping others and educating them. From that day on, I realized that honest transparency was powerful. Knowing that someone knew what I was going through helped me grow and mature.

That's what I pray you got from this book. I pray that you go away with a sense of purpose, with a vision and a goal of what kind of man you want to be; what kind of legacy you want to leave behind. I pray that your eyes have been opened even more to your calling. I pray that you take what you learned from me and go out and share it.

Everything in this book was purposed to point you back to Jesus. He is our everything. He is our answer. The Bible has every answer to life. Even if you got one thing from this book, that's cool with me. I am not a professional writer, but I wanted to share what God has put in my heart over the years. Men, it's time to go beyond casual Christianity and break free from hypocrisy in the Church. It's time to wake up and become the men God is calling us to be.

PRAYER

Whether you know God intimately or not, I encourage you to pray this prayer of rededication. Maybe you pray something like this every day, or maybe this is your first time doing anything like this. Please, take this time to speak this out loud. God hears you, whether you whisper this or shout it out loud.

God, I want to take this time to thank you for this moment. In this very moment, I am alive and I have purpose. I may not know the full plan of my life in detail, but You do. You have a purpose for me. God, forgive me of my past mistakes. Forgive me of all my sins I have committed. This very moment is a chance to start over. I acknowledge what your Son, Jesus Christ, did for me on the cross. I acknowledge that He gave His life for me so that I can be forgiven. I acknowledge that I was guilty of unrighteousness, but Jesus took my punishment and gave me His righteousness. I thank you for this opportunity to start fresh, no matter what I have done.

God, I want to be better. I want to live the life you are calling me to live. I want to be a better man, a better husband, a better son, a better brother, and a better person. I ask, in the name of Jesus, that you change me, teach me, correct me, and discipline me, so that I can become a true man of God.

No matter what people say, or what people think of me, I choose to live for you. I choose to love. I choose to encourage. I choose to surrender my entire life to you and your will. I give you full control of my life, and I confess you as my Lord and Savior. I confess you as my God.

I thank you, God, for washing my past mistakes away. I thank you for cleaning me, healing me, forgiving me, and making me a new creation in Christ Jesus. From this point forward, change me. Change my thinking, change my words, and change my reasoning. God, use me to expand your Kingdom. In Jesus' name I pray, amen.

#DearChristianMen

INFLUENCES

There were many amazing men (and women) of God who influenced me throughout my entire Christian walk, especially while writing this book. Their passion and zeal for God inspired me to dive deeper and deeper into God's Word.

James Mark Driscoll
Pastor of Grace by Faith Life Church
Clarinda, IA.

**Dave Legget, Anette Wagoner,
And Tony Ramaeker**
Pastors of New Life Fellowship
Council Bluffs, IA.

Fabian McCune
Pastor of Vital Church
Columbus, GA.

Keith Moore
Pastor of Faith Life Church
Branson, MO.

Judah Smith
Pastor of The City Church
Seattle, WA.

Cornelius Lindsey
Pastor of The Gathering Oasis
Atlanta, GA.

Ryan LeStrange
Ryan LeStrange Ministries
Bristol, VA

And
Francis Chan

#DearChristianMen

NOTES

Chapter 3

[1] *"Tetelestai* (It Is Finished)" "Greek Lexicon :: G5055 (KJV)." Blue Letter Bible, 2 May, 2015. https://www.blueletterbible.org/lang/lexicon/lexicon.cfm?Strongs=G5055

Chapter 4

[2] Refresh Ministries. (2013, June 28). *God is Better- Francis Chan Sermon Jam.* [Video File]. Retrieved from https://www.youtube.com/watch?v=W-pLRM0rgjE. Original Sermon by Francis Chan.

Chapter 6

[3] Refresh Ministries. (2013, June 3). *Hosea and Gomer- Judah Smith Sermon Jam.* [Video File]. Retrieved from https://www.youtube.com/watch?v=r1DxoJqdopY. Original sermon by Judah Smith.

Chapter 7

[4] "Prevail." *Dictionary.com Unabridged.* Random House, Inc. 04 May. 2015. <Dictionary.com http://dictionary.reference.com/browse/prevail>.

[5] Men's Devotional Bible by Zondervan. (2012, September 25). *YouVersion: Men's Devotional: For Men, By Men: Day 1. "The Full Eight Seconds.* https://www.bible.com/reading-plans/1047-mens-devotional-for-men-by-men/day/1

Chapter 9

[6] "Hamartolos (sinner)" "Greek Lexicon :: G268 (KJV)." Blue Letter Bible, 1 May, 2015. http://www.blueletterbible.org/lang/lexicon/lexicon.cfm?Strongs=G268

[7] "Hagios (saint)" "Greek Lexicon :: G40 (NASB)." Blue Letter Bible, 9 May, 2015. https://www.blueletterbible.org/lang/lexicon/lexicon.cfm?Strongs=G40

#DearChristianMen

#DearChristianMen

www.ingramcontent.com/pod-product-compliance
Lightning Source LLC
Chambersburg PA
CBHW060012050426
42448CB00012B/2722